ON A BACKYARD SAFARI

WITH OUR FATHER OF DETAILS

© 2016 by TGS International, a wholly owned subsidiary of
Christian Aid Ministries, Berlin, Ohio.

All rights reserved. No part of this book may be used, reproduced, or stored in any retrieval system, in any form or by any means, electronic or mechanical, without written permission from the publisher except for brief quotations embodied in critical articles and reviews.

ISBN: 978-1-943929-13-9

Cover photos: Mike Atnip

Cover design: Kristi Yoder

Interior design: Teresa Sommers

Photographs in this book by Mike and Daniel Atnip unless credited otherwise on page 192.

Printed in China

Published by:
TGS International
P.O. Box 355, Berlin, Ohio 44610 USA
Phone: 330-893-4828
Fax: 330-893-2305
www.tgsinternational.com

TGS001247

ON A BACKYARD SAFARI

WITH OUR FATHER OF DETAILS

MIKE ATNIP

The Journey

The word *safari* is an English adaption of an African Swahili word meaning "journey." This journal is a record of an incredible safari my family and I made in the last year. We invite you to join us on this safari for a small glimpse of the majesty of our Father of details.

We will begin with a vantage point that shows the universe somewhat as God might see it, except that our perspective is always incomplete. While our Father of details sees infinity, we humans are limited. Our minds want to "blow a fuse" when we try to imagine the vastness of outer space. So we have to start with the visible universe, that which we can see and measure. The photo on this page encompasses one tiny slice of that universe—an area of night sky equivalent to a pinhead held at arm's length.

Astronomers estimate that the most distant objects observable with the most powerful telescopes today are around 13 billion (13,000,000,000) light-years away, and that the universe is at least several times larger than that. Within that incomprehensible expanse are an estimated 300 sextillion (300,000,000,000,000,000,000,000) stars in 130 billion (130,000,000,000) galaxies.

Now let's narrow our field of view.

This galaxy is similar to the Milky Way, the one in which we float. But several hundred billion stars are still far too many to focus on, so we will choose just one speck in the Milky Way: our sun with its planets.

In fact, we will limit ourselves to planet Earth for our peek into the majesty of our Father of details. But even Earth, a tiny detail in the vastness of the observable universe, is far too big for our study.

Our Two ACRES

We've chosen two acres on Earth—just two from among its 36,677,592,320 acres of land. A portion of these two acres is visible in the bird's-eye photo, from the foreground to where the two buggies are parked against the white shed near the upper middle of the photo.

At first glance nothing here seems remarkable. These two acres contain no jungle, no rushing rivers, not even a gurgling creek or a picturesque pond. There is a house, several outbuildings, a garden, a small pasture, a tiny woods (right side, back corner), and some fruit trees—all within the small town of New Bedford, Ohio.

What kind of surprises could God have in a two-acre town lot? What can we find on our safari?

Our First Surprise

A bumblebee is foraging on the head of an onion plant in one of the gardens. Perhaps you are thinking there is nothing outstanding about a bumblebee in a garden, but let's stop a moment and examine this bee. Turn the page to see . . .

Don't forget to notice the three *ocelli* (simple eyes) between the two compound eyes!

. . . A BUMBLEBEE UP CLOSE.

Consider the many details that make up a "simple" bumblebee. Examine its soft hair, neatly trimmed as if it has just come from a barbershop; its large eyes, which give it a view in practically any direction to the front; its neat knee joints; the hairs on its legs; the antennae.

All these details, and each one has a purpose. But let's look closer yet at the foot of the bumblebee on the next page.

Imagine a bumblebee without any hooks on its feet! Would it be able to hang on to flowers if it were clawless? Our Father of details considered the bumblebee carefully when He designed it!

Not Enough Books

The Apostle John wrote in his gospel that "there are also many other things which Jesus did, the which, if they should be written every one, I suppose that even the world itself could not contain the books that should be written. Amen" (John 21:25).

John may have been referring only to those things Jesus did while incarnate on earth, or he may also have been including Jesus' participation in the creation of the world. As a boy, I wondered if John was not stretching things a bit to say the world could not contain the books about the things Jesus did. I no longer doubt that statement. Think of the vastness of the universe, and think of that little detail—one detail among trillions—of the bumblebee foot we just looked at.

A whole book could be written about a bumblebee foot: how it formed in the egg, how the claws are moved by tiny muscles, how the bee's brain sends electronic signals to those muscles to precisely control the timing and degree with which the claw opens and grasps. Beyond that, one could study how the claws are formed of atoms, and how molecules bond together to form the needed substances—some hard, some soft, some bonding strongly to surrounding tissue (muscle to ligaments), some not bonding (blood to artery). Most likely, swarms of bacteria and viruses, invisible to the human eye, are living on that bumblebee foot.

Indeed, several books could be written about a bumblebee foot! Yet that foot is just one little detail in an immense universe planned by our Father of details. He considers the needs of bumblebees and cares for the sparrows, and He counts the number of hairs on our heads. Yes, John was correct; the world could not contain the books that could be written about the majesty and glory of Jesus and our Father of details!

This journal is just an introduction to that majesty, like peering at one grain of sand on a seashore. The number of species of living things in existence (plant, animal, and microbial) is estimated at eight or nine million, but that is just an educated guess. This journal is meant to encourage children (and adults) that one does not need to go on exotic safaris or visit far-off jungles to find unique and intriguing creatures. They inhabit our houses and yards. All we have to do is look!

Every species documented in this book lives on our two-acre lot. Each one (with a few exceptions, which are noted) has been photographed by Mike or Daniel Atnip, two ordinary people on an ordinary town lot in Ohio. Let's go! Join our safari into the majesty and glory of our Father of details!

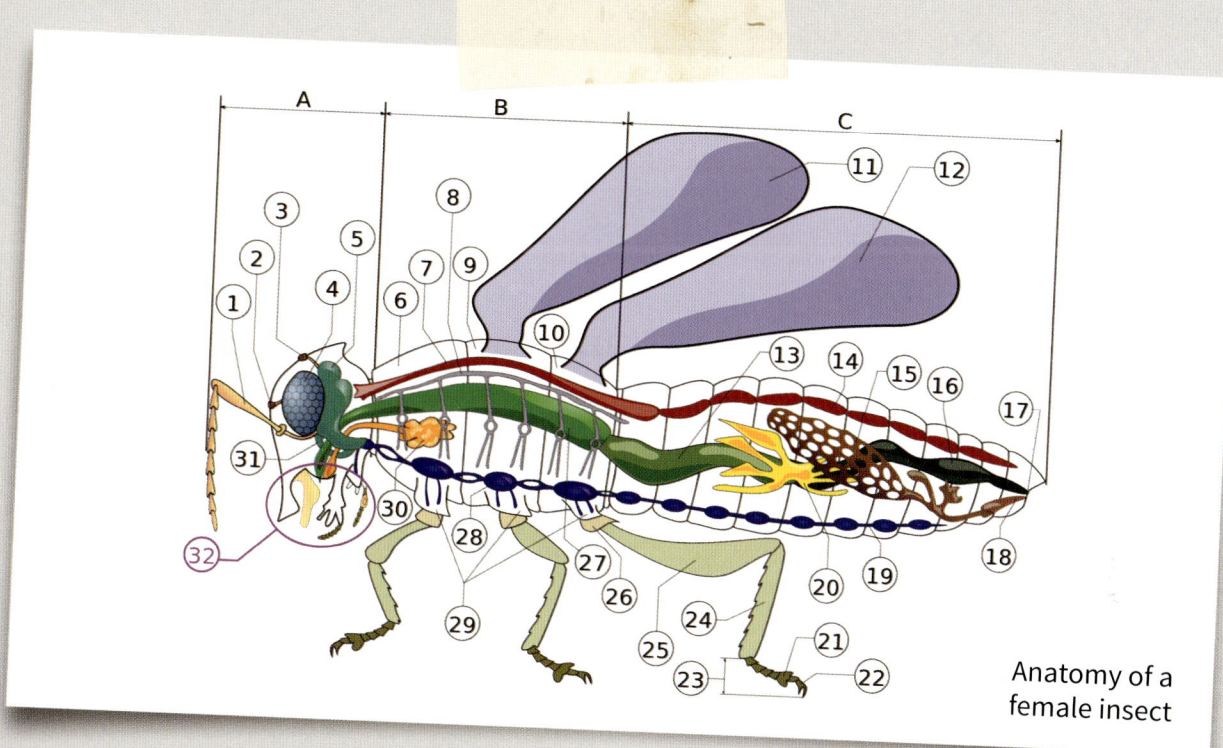

Anatomy of a female insect

In·sect: Having Sections

Insects got their name for a simple reason: they have three body sections! If a critter doesn't have three body sections, it is not an insect. Spiders, for example, have only two body sections. Turn the page to meet our first insect species.

Insect Anatomy Key

A- Head B- Thorax C- Abdomen 1. antenna 2. ocelli (lower) 3. ocelli (upper) 4. compound eye 5. brain 6. prothorax 7. dorsal artery 8. tracheal tubes 9. mesothorax 10. metathorax 11. first wing 12. second wing 13. midgut 14. heart 15. ovary 16. hindgut 17. anus 18. vagina 19. nerve cord 20. Malpighian tubes 21. pillow 22. claws 23. tarsus 24. tibia 25. femur 26. trochanter 27. foregut 28. thoracic ganglion 29. coxa 30. salivary gland 31. subesophageal ganglion 32. mouthparts

An Ugly Ol' Grasshopper?

Our Father of details gave this road duster awesome leg muscles for leaping again, and again, and again. He gave him wings to fly a little, although he will never soar high into the heavens like an eagle. But did God give him any beauty? Turn the page to see!

SPECIES #1

KINGDOM: Animalia
PHYLUM: Arthropoda
CLASS: Insecta
ORDER: Orthoptera
FAMILY: Acrididae
GENUS: *Dissosteira*
SPECIES: *carolina*

Locust or Grasshopper?

Do you know the difference between a locust and a grasshopper? I didn't.

For hundreds of years, grasshoppers and locusts were thought to be different species, but on further study, scientists found that certain species of grasshoppers change color and behavior when they become too numerous in an area. Then they go into emigration mode and swarm away, eating any (and often every) leafy green thing in their path.

The species pictured here is commonly called the **Carolina grasshopper** or Carolina locust. Other common names include black-winged grasshopper, Quaker locust, or road duster grasshopper. This last name comes from these grasshoppers' liking for dusty, pebbly areas, like roadside ditches, for which they have been perfectly camouflaged by our Father of details. This camouflage is important, since nearly all predators, including humans, eat grasshoppers. A hungry wild turkey can walk right over one of these, thinking it is just another pebble. Of the 11,000 species of grasshoppers, the Carolina grasshopper is one of the least destructive.

And those wings! Daniel came into the house exclaiming that he had just caught a butterfly. When I looked at it, I immediately shook my head and said, "That's not a butterfly; that's a grasshopper!" *Come on, Daniel, you should know better than that!*

"No, it's a butterfly. Watch him fly!" I was reluctant to let him turn the "thing" loose in the house, but he declared he could catch it again. However, it refused to do more than just a short hop.

Later as I prepared it for drying, I started to position it with a typical "wings closed" position. However, Daniel insisted that I open its wings. It was a bit of a "wow" moment to pull open those large "butterfly" wings, folded neatly accordion-wise and hidden by the dull front wings. No wonder Daniel thought it was a butterfly!

Later I found that reference guides say this species appears to be a butterfly when hovering. The male grasshopper rises above the ground and hovers for up to fifteen seconds, looking for a mate. While this hovering is not fully understood, it seems to be a courting pattern. The female lays her eggs in loose soil, where the eggs overwinter and hatch in the spring. Destructive locust plagues have decreased in some parts of the world, and some researchers believe this is because widespread soil tillage destroys many grasshopper eggs.

Note: The drying process causes color loss in insects, so this specimen is duller than when it was alive. Keep this in mind as you journey through this book and see other photos of dried specimens.

SPECIES #2

KINGDOM: Animalia
PHYLUM: Arthropoda
CLASS: Insecta
ORDER: Lepidoptera
FAMILY: Nymphalidae
GENUS: *Danaus*
SPECIES: *plexippus*

King of Butterflies

In the American Midwest, the sight of a **monarch butterfly** on a summer day is one of those amazing details we almost take for granted. Our neighbor had a butterfly bush, *Buddleja davidii* (also known as summer lilac or orange eye), just a few feet from our property. These bushes live up to their name, and this one attracted some monarchs. Daniel wanted to add one to our collection, but in keeping with our goal of only collecting species on our two acres, I told him it was off limits. Besides, the neighbors may not have appreciated us swiping monarchs from their property. It was tempting, though, to chase one over the line!

Not many days later, I happened to look out our kitchen window at our own butterfly bush to see a monarch feeding. "Daniel! There's a monarch on our butterfly bush!" In seconds he had risen from the table, dashed for the net, and bolted out the door. Within a minute or so, he was back with our prize.

This specimen is a male, distinguished by narrower black veins on the wings and two spots called **androconia** on its hind wings. The androconia in some butterfly species release **pheromones**, which are hormonal secretions, or scents. Pheromones attract mates, send alarm signals, and communicate other messages, such as the trail to a food supply. We are only beginning to discover the varied uses of pheromones. Interestingly, the androconia on monarchs do not appear to release pheromones.

Besides their ornate beauty, God has given this species a matchless trait: the ability to return to their exact wintering grounds (sometimes just a few acres) hundreds or thousands of miles away, even though they have never been there before. That's right. The monarchs that leave their Central or South American wintering grounds never return, but their children or grandchildren return to the same spot! In one study, commercially bred monarchs returned to the same wintering grounds as their forefathers—after nine generations in captivity! Did our Father of details give monarchs a built-in GPS system?

Monarch larvae feed on milkweed, which provides chemicals that make them taste bad to predators. Thus, monarchs have few predators and rarely get eaten. They can freely flutter about, amazing us with their God-given ability to return to their grandparents' wintering grounds without Dad or Grandpa showing them the way.

Orange Crowns

In this photo taken at the Monarch Butterfly Reserve, Michoacan, Mexico, oodles of monarchs cling to the branches of stately trees. They will head north when spring warms the northern hemisphere.

SPECIES #3

KINGDOM: Animalia
PHYLUM: Arthropoda
CLASS: Insecta
ORDER: Lepidoptera
FAMILY: Papilionidae
GENUS: *Papilio*
SPECIES: *glaucu*

Flying Tiger

It has the tail of a swallow and tiger stripes on its wings. As a caterpillar, in the first three *instars*, or stages of development between molts, it looks like a bird dropping. Then, in the last two instars, it has two large eyespots to scare off predators. Besides the two fake eyes, it also has an ***osmeterium***, a little set of "horns" that protrudes from its head. Not only do these make the caterpillar look larger and more like a snake, they also emit a foul odor.

In beauty the **tiger swallowtail** rivals the monarch butterfly. The female sports contrasting bluish colors on the tips of her rear wings. The specimen pictured here is a male.

Male swallowtails exhibit a behavior known as ***puddling***. You may have noticed a group of butterflies gathered on a damp area of soil or a food source. They are sucking up the moisture, not necessarily for a drink of water, but to gather nutrients. Some puddling species pass enormous amounts of fluid through their digestive systems—up to six hundred times their own body mass, yielding far more nutrients than a single drink would give. In some species, the male then passes some of the collected nutrients to the female. Who but our Father of details would have designed such a unique way for the male to gather nutrients for the family!

We learned the hard way that butterfly wings are especially fragile. Since we had caught many of our insects with plastic peanut butter containers, when we netted these swallowtail butterflies, we transferred them to those same containers until we could dry them. We soon found out that a peanut butter container is too small for a butterfly. It flops around, beating off its wings and scales. Not only does it destroy the beauty of the specimen, but it is unkind to keep a large-winged insect in a container where it strikes the walls with every flap of its wings. A five-quart ice cream bucket preserves the wings of captive butterflies much better!

Leaping Propagation

If this book inspires you to go on your own backyard safari, I hope you do not find members of this species! If you do, you had better begin considering measures to counter their spread. A **dog flea** can live several months without eating, but the female has to have a meal of blood before she can produce eggs. Don't worry, though; they rarely bite humans!

Although they have no wings, some fleas can jump two hundred times their body length, and they can jump six hundred times an hour nonstop for three days in search of a host to live on! Once they find a host, all those spiny hairs on their body parts help them navigate among the host's hairs. The fleas are flat laterally, meaning they look a little like a piece of brown paper standing on edge. This flatness permits them to squeeze into tight places, an ideal ability for a life among hairs.

When the female starts laying eggs, she can put out about 4,000 of them. These will hatch and become adults within two or three weeks. Let's do some math and see how one flea could become a multitude very quickly. For simplicity, we will round the generation cycle to one month.

- First month = 1 flea
- Second month = 4,000 fleas
- Third month = 8,000,000 fleas (assuming half of the 4,000 were males)
- Fourth month = 16,000,000,000 fleas (assuming half of the 8,000,000 were males)

You can see now why I hope you don't find even one of this species in your backyard! Thankfully, not all the eggs will hatch and develop, so by the fourth month you may find only one billion fleas rather than sixteen billion.

While dog fleas also infests cats, raccoons, opossums, and other animals, there are also cat fleas and human fleas, which are separate species. The Black Death was spread in Europe in the Middle Ages by fleas on rats. These fleas carried the *Yersinia pestis* bacteria, which eventually killed 30 to 60 percent of the European population. Truly, little things—like fleas carrying bacteria—can confound the wise!

A cat flea has a less rounded head than a dog flea and only six notches on its back legs, whereas dog fleas have eight. To complicate matters, cat fleas—which are more common than dog fleas—also infest dogs. We identified this specimen as a dog flea because of its more rounded head. (And yes, it did come from our dog, who has now been treated with a commercial product in hopes of eradicating this flea species from our property.)

Fleas can go into *diapause*, a dormant state that can be broken when the sleepy flea senses heat, vibrations, or a rise in

Note that this flea is covered with super glue to prop it up for photos. In the corner is a small front view to show how flat a flea's body is from side to side.

SPECIES #4

KINGDOM: Animalia
PHYLUM: Arthropoda
CLASS: Insecta
ORDER: Siphonaptera
FAMILY: Pulicidae
GENUS: *Ctenocephalides*
SPECIES: *canis*

carbon dioxide that signals the approach of a potential host.

I know of nothing positive that fleas contribute to this world other than to present some amazing details that cause us to worship our Father of details and admire His skill. He certainly did an excellent job of equipping the flea to live in the hairy places of this earth.

The Scissor Song

Though this insect is commonly called a **scissor grinder locust** in reference to its "song," it is neither a locust nor a grasshopper! Other common names include dryfly, greenback dryfly, July-fly, jar-fly, Pharaoh bug, dog day cicada (from its appearance during the "dog days" of late July and August), and harvest fly.

We tentatively identified the specimen on this page as species *pruinosus*, but I will readily admit (along with identification guides) that it could be one of several other closely related species, such as *winnemanna*, *latifasciatus*, or even a hybrid. While the anatomy of the related species is similar, each "sings" a slightly different tune. The *Tibicen* genus appears every year, though they have a multi-year life cycle, while the related thirteen-year and seventeen-year genera (plural of genus) appear sporadically. And yes, the seventeen-year cicada actually appears every seventeen years, though different broods are on different cycles so that most years a brood hatches somewhere.

Some species of cicadas can whine at more than a hundred decibels, equal to the noise of a small engine or motorcycle. I can clearly remember living near Cambridge, Ohio, in 1999 when the seventeen-year cicadas hatched there. We were living in a little cabin at the edge of a woods, and the singing was *loud!* Cicadas were crawling out of the ground and hanging onto trees everywhere. Digging into the ground, we saw their tunnels as they made their way up from the six-foot depth where they spend most of their lives before emerging in their final year.

To reveal my ignorance once again, it was not until we found this specimen on our property that I even knew there were "annual" cicadas. (With a lifecycle of two or three years, these are not truly annual either. They appear annually because, like the seventeen-year cicadas, different broods come out in different years.)

Male cicadas have an area on the abdomen called a *tymbal*, with rib-like structures they pull in and out to make a click. The abdomens of cicadas are mostly hollow, providing a sound box. By twisting their abdomens a bit, cicadas can vary the tones they create. Doing this rapidly produces a sound like a power saw cutting through wood (species *linnei*) or like scissors being sharpened (species *pruinosus*); hence the name *scissor grinder*. Each cicada recognizes the unique song of its own species. The male and female use the songs to locate one another.

Cicadas spend most of their lives one to eight feet underground, the depth depending on the species. There they feed on xylem in root sap. Emerging years later, they crawl up any handy support and emerge from their final instar as winged adults. The female then lays her eggs in slits she makes in tree branches. The eggs hatch, the nymphs drop to the ground, and the underground stage of their life begins anew.

In designing this lifecycle, our Father of details may have had something more in mind than cicada propagation. When the female makes her slits in tree branches, some of the branches end up dying from the damage. One entomologist claims this is a natural pruning process, and that fruit trees may produce more fruit the year after a big cicada emergence. I suppose that would be a good science project for an organic orchard—but don't blame me if it doesn't work!

With over 2,500 described species worldwide and more waiting to be described, cicadas are found everywhere except Antarctica. In some parts of the world they are prized as a delicacy, with the females being preferred, as they are said to be "meatier." A recipe for German Chocolate Cicada Cake calls for fifty blanched female cicadas. Personally, I prefer my cakes without insects; I confess I am a wimp when it comes to trying new foods!

SPECIES #5

KINGDOM: Animalia
PHYLUM: Arthropoda
CLASS: Insecta
ORDER: Hemiptera
FAMILY: Cicadidae
GENUS: *Tibicen*
SPECIES: *pruinosus?*

This cicada shell intrigued me so much that I had to include a photo of it in this journal. Check out the details—the tongue, the legs, and even the hairs on its eyes!

SPIRITUAL LESSON

The maturing cicada had to escape from this "prison" to keep maturing. So the Christian must keep growing "from glory to glory" lest he also stagnate and die, confined in the prison of lukewarmness, formality, and complacency!

SPECIES #6

KINGDOM: Animalia
PHYLUM: Arthropoda
CLASS: Insecta
ORDER: Lepidoptera
FAMILY: Geometridae
GENUS:
SPECIES:

Earth Measurers

The **geometer moths** get their family name from their "inchworm" caterpillars. These little creatures move along, arching and extending their bodies, about an inch at a time. To an observer, they give the appearance of trying to "measure the earth." Hence the name *geometer*—*geo* is Greek for "earth," and *meter* means "measure." You will notice we've given this one no genus or species names: we simply could not identify the species.

A·rach·no·pho·bi·a:
{Fear of spiders}

Remember the nursery rhyme about Miss Muffet?

Little Miss Muffet sat on her tuffet,
Eating her curds and whey.
Along came a spider and sat down beside her,
And frightened Miss Muffet away.

I am now a recovering arachnophobe. Except for the past half year of my life, I considered spiders my enemies and generally killed without pity any spider that crawled into my path or built a web in what I considered my space. Perhaps this attitude stemmed from the mistaken belief that many spiders are deadly poisonous, and from my childhood exposure to Miss Muffet.

Why would any mother repeat such words to her darling baby, if not to instill arachnophobia in the next generation? Let's look at a revised version:

Little Miss Muffet sat on her tuffet,
Eating her curds and whey.
Along came a spider and sat down beside her,
And gladdened Miss Muffet's new day.

Let's consider the truth about spiders. As a starting point, guess how many people per year, on average, die from proven spider bites. If you guessed about one per year, you are correct. Your chances of being killed by lightning are twenty-five times greater! You are fifteen times more likely to die from a jellyfish sting than a spider bite. Finally, consider that you are 40,000 times more likely to die in an auto accident than from a spider bite.

Perhaps you argue that while not many people die from spider bites, thousands get sick from spider bites every year. Let's consider that point of view. In the mid-1900s, a medical report was released about how the brown recluse spider was venomous, potentially causing sickness and death in humans. News media spread the report widely. Suddenly, over the next decades, tens of thousands of people reported sickness from brown recluse spider bites.

What's interesting is that many of these reports came from areas outside the known range of brown recluse spiders. For example, in South Carolina over twelve hundred cases of sickness from brown recluse bites were recorded in fourteen years. The problem with that number is that, except for the very western edge of the state, brown recluses are not found in South Carolina! A grand total of forty-five brown recluse specimens have been documented in western South Carolina.

On the other hand, a famous Kansas study gathered 2,055 brown recluse specimens from one house. I confess that if I lived in a house with that many brown recluse spiders, I would seriously consider moving! But the family of four who lived in the house had reported no bites in six years. After eleven years, the mother of the family reported being bitten by a spider when she reached into a shirt sleeve in the laundry. Spiders only bite in self-defense, and this one was most likely trapped in the sleeve with no escape route. The woman's bitten finger turned red and swelled a little but healed without incident.

On rare occasions when spiders do bite humans, the bite is usually about as severe as a bee sting. Most incidents of reported spider bite sicknesses are not verified spider bites at all. For example, a person who finds a red spot on his skin may remember seeing a spider in the last day or two and conclude, with no evidence, that the spider bit him. More than forty different infections cause sores similar to spider bites, and research has shown that most "spider bites" are actually infected spots on the skin that have nothing to do with spiders.

So, are spiders dangerous? Can you die from a spider bite? Yes, it is possible to die from a spider bite. However, it is more rational to save your worries for jellyfish, lightning bolts, and car rides, any of which will kill you sooner than a spider will!

Remember, throughout the twentieth century, spider bites killed only one person per year. During that same century, spiders consumed billions and billions of potentially destructive insects. Spiders are our friends, our helpers, and our free local exterminators, feasting on insects (e.g. mosquitoes, flies, grasshoppers, moths, and cockroaches) that spread diseases and destroy crops.

If you would like to join me in recovering from arachnophobia, please turn the page and meet one of your new friends face to face.

Daniel's zebra jumping spider navigating the hairs on the back of his hand. If you keep jumping spiders as pets, as Daniel does, don't try to keep more than one in a jar. As Daniel learned the hard way, they will eat each other.

SPECIES #7

KINGDOM: Animalia
PHYLUM: Arthropoda
CLASS: Arachnida
ORDER: Araneae
FAMILY: Salticidae
GENUS: *Salticus*
SPECIES: *scenicus*

Striped Actor

Zebra jumping spiders have stripes—like a zebra. This species is a member of the jumping spider family, with the typical traits. But take a look at the species name. *Scenicus* is a Latin word related to *scenes*, as in theater scenes. *Scenicus* earned its name from its theatrical behavior when approached by humans. Even though they eat one another, zebra jumping spiders can act comical, almost like monkeys!

This species is adept at stalking prey. The receptors in its eyes give it depth perception to accurately reckon when the time has come to make the final lunge after a long, careful stalk.

The leap happens too fast to capture it in sixty frames per second.

While soaring through the air, a jumping spider is moving at about two feet per second, and some species can jump fifty times their own body length. If humans could jump like that in proportion to their size, a six-foot man could jump three hundred feet to grab a rabbit for supper!

Jumping is not the only amazing ability of the jumping spiders. After we learned about them, Daniel wanted one for a pet. Since the first one had been killed for photos, he made a search and found another one. I gave him permission to keep it in the house, with a strong warning not to let it escape. You guessed it—the little spider somehow escaped.

A few days later I was lying on the couch and happened to notice it crawling along the ceiling. "Daniel," I hollered, "there's your jumping spider." When Daniel reached up with a jar to capture it, the little spider, right before my eyes, dropped from the ceiling to the floor, spinning a dragline behind it—all in about one second! In that time it had spit out the end of the dragline from its **spinnerets**, attached it to the ceiling, and dropped eight feet to the floor, a distance of two hundred times its own body length. (Jumping spiders usually spin a dragline when jumping, allowing them to simply crawl back up if the jump doesn't end well.) This would be the equivalent of a man attaching the end of a rope to an anchor point and dropping twelve hundred feet, spinning the rope as he fell—not to mention crawling quickly back up if necessary!

Of course, the jumping spider I saw on the ceiling was walking upside down. I have also seen one walking on a sheet of paper held in Daniel's hand. When it came to the edge, it simply continued its walk around the edge of the paper and onto the bottom side as if nothing had happened. Jumping spiders can even climb the side of a glass jar or hang upside down on its lid while resting. In addition to the standard two claws most spiders have, jumping spiders are blessed with an extra tuft of thick hair that serves as a third claw.

The bold jumping spider is just one of more than 5,000 species in the jumping spider family. The Latin root of the species name, *audax*, is easily recognized as the root for our English word *audacious*. It's a good name. They are indeed brave little creatures! When you approach a bold jumping spider, the spider will likely turn to face you. Extend your hand slowly and carefully toward it, and it may well jump onto your hand to inspect it. More than once I have seen one hop onto an approaching camera lens.

Jumping spiders are carnivorous, which means that almost anything that moves may qualify as a meal. Some species have been known to approach the web of a funnel spider, move slowly to the edge, and jiggle the web lightly. When the funnel spider rushes out, expecting to subdue and

eat the trapped prey, the jumping spider attacks the funnel spider and eats it. It is truly a spider-eat-spider world out there!

The Salticidae family are well-studied spiders. They comprise about 13 percent of all the spider species, making them the largest family of spiders. Their distinctiveness and delightful antics may be the reason more people have chosen to study them rather than more mundane species.

The jumping spiders have very good eyesight for spiders. Tests show that they can discern and respond to individual colors. Although their eyes are too close together to detect depth the way humans do, jumping spiders do have depth perception based on four receptors in the back of the eye. Light falls in focus on one receptor and out of focus on the others, allowing the spider to perceive depth and distance.

When stalking prey, jumping spiders sometimes sneak around, perhaps crawling down one limb and up another, following the prey even if they lose sight of it temporarily. They may crawl to a point above the prey and do the drop-on-a-dragline trick or swing out in an arc on a tethered line. All these amazing skills are given to them by our Father of details!

Each frame below is 1/60 of a second. From resting to takeoff, this zebra jumping spider needs only six frames, about 1/10 of a second! In this frame you can see the blur as the spider speeds away.

Safari Woes

During our safari, species identification sometimes eluded our best efforts. Which of the more than 5,000 jumping spider species is dining on that fruit fly Daniel fed him?

See those neat, steely irises in the photo below? After admiring them for several days, I was lying in bed one night when it hit me: *Those are probably reflections of the camera lens, not irises!* Sure enough, upon investigation, I found that those compelling "irises" were not irises after all.

SPECIES #9

KINGDOM: Animalia
PHYLUM: Arthropoda
CLASS: Arachnida
ORDER: Araneae
FAMILY: Salticidae
GENUS:
SPECIES:

> **SPECIES #10**
>
> **KINGDOM:** Animalia
> **PHYLUM:** Arthropoda
> **CLASS:** Insecta
> **ORDER:** Lepidoptera
> **FAMILY:** Noctuidae
> **GENUS:** *Helicoverpa*
> **SPECIES:** *zea*

King of the Cob

If you grow sweet corn, consider yourself blessed if you shuck your supper and do not find a **corn earworm** crawling on the tip. Usually only one worm is found per ear, not because the moth laid only a single egg per ear, but because the little larvae are as nasty to their brothers and sisters as they are to the tip of the corn: they are cannibals! And these hungry caterpillars' appetite extends well beyond corn and other earworms—the species also goes by the common names of tomato fruitworm, cotton bollworm, vetchworm, and sorghum headworm.

Corn earworm eggs usually hatch several days after they are laid. The larvae go through four to six instars as they mature. Once they are through all the instars, they dig themselves two to four inches into the soil, where they pupate for about two weeks. After they become moths, they live an average of only two more weeks. It's a short lifespan, but our Father of details gave the female earworm moths an average of a thousand eggs to lay. He gave the earworm the ability to go through diapause, which means "delayed development due to adverse environmental conditions." He also made the moths excellent flyers, able to be carried as far as three hundred miles on the wind. No wonder corn earworms spread so well!

We did not find any corn earworm moths on our safari, but the tiny picture above the larva is added to give you an idea of what these little cannibals look like as adults.

These blue hawker dragonfly photos are not from our safari. However, they provide an excellent example of incomplete metamorphosis.

Metamorphosis

Metamorphosis is a Greek compound of *meta*, meaning "change," and *morphosis*, meaning "form"—a "change of form." Two types of metamorphosis exist in insects and spiders:

- *Hemimetabolous,* or incomplete metamorphosis. In this type of metamorphosis, the changes are gradual, with no drastic change from one phase to the next. The immature stages are called nymphs or instars. Nymphs pass through multiple instars to become adults.
- *Holometabolous*, or complete metamorphosis. In this type of metamorphosis, a total and radical change of form occurs in one step. The immature form is called the larva. Larvae live for a time and then enter a temporary resting stage in the form of a pupa (or chrysalis). Often the pupa is inside a silk cocoon, but not always. The adult emerges from the pupa. One common example of this type of metamorphosis is the change of a caterpillar into a butterfly.

Some species experience both complete and incomplete metamorphosis.

44

SPIRITUAL LESSON

Did you know Christians experience metamorphosis? Romans 12:2 tells us, "And be not conformed to this world: but be ye transformed [metamorphosized] by the renewing of your mind, that ye may prove what is that good, and acceptable, and perfect, will of God." Like the caterpillar crawling in the dirt, we humans crawl in our carnal appetites until our Father of details calls us to heavenly places. How can a caterpillar fly in the heavens? How can a human live in heavenly places? By experiencing metamorphosis!

Jesus told us in John 3:3, "Verily, verily, I say unto thee, Except a man be born again, he cannot see the kingdom of God." This tells us that we cannot be part of the kingdom Jesus came to establish on earth unless our Father of details sends us His Spirit to remake our inner man (both our thinking and our attitudes). This is a complete metamorphosis of spirit, in contrast to the mere bodily metamorphosis of an insect.

As we walk with Jesus, we will also experience *incomplete* metamorphosis. 2 Corinthians 3:18 tells us, "But we all, with open face beholding as in a glass the glory of the Lord, are changed into the same image from glory to glory, even as by the Spirit of the Lord." The phrase *changed into* is once again the Greek word *metamorphosized!* This describes the progress of the believer as he grows in the knowledge of God. While many of the changes in a believer's life are subtle and incremental, there will also be positive and noticeable growth spurts, like an insect's changes from one instar to the next.

For those who remain faithful to the end, there will be yet another metamorphosis, a metamorphosis of the body. I cannot offer a detailed description of the new body since we haven't experienced it yet. We eagerly await the time when, like the butterfly, we enter a totally new existence, a change we can only imagine now. Meanwhile, we experience the first metamorphosis of our inner man.

Singing Legs

Do you suffer from ragweed allergies? If so, this common **differential grasshopper**, normally considered a pest, could be your friend. Yes, it eats ragweed! The unusual black V-shaped chevron markings on its rear legs can help identify this species, although a few other species have these marks as well.

Differential grasshoppers tend to live in swarms. Each female lays up to several hundred eggs in soft soil. The eggs overwinter and hatch the following spring. Even starting with a swarm of only a few hundred females, imagine the number of grasshopper nymphs crawling out of the ground the next spring!

Differential grasshoppers sing, or *stridulate*, by rubbing the pegs on their rear legs against their wings—imagine rubbing your fingernails over a washboard. In contrast, crickets and katydids stridulate by rubbing their wings together. Another interesting difference between these insects is in the location of their *tympanum,* a hearing organ sometimes called an eardrum, though it has a different structure and function. In grasshoppers the tympanum is on the abdomen, while in crickets and katydids it is on the knee of the front leg. So grasshoppers sing with their legs and hear with their bellies, while crickets and katydids sing with their wings and hear with their legs!

Dead grasshoppers and katydids lose their green color within a couple of days, turning a bland dark brown, so if you want to photograph your collected specimens, plan to do it as soon as you can.

On the opposite page you can see a close-up of a grasshopper "ear." The picture above shows where this tympanum is located on a differential grasshopper.

SPECIES #11

KINGDOM: Animalia
PHYLUM: Arthropoda
CLASS: Insecta
ORDER: Orthoptera
FAMILY: Acrididae
GENUS: *Melanoplus*
SPECIES: *differentialis*

Clouded Identity

There are eighty species in the genus *Colias;* which species did we find? I opted for *philodice*, based on identification photos that matched closely. However, a couple of the other species were also close in coloration. Throw in the hybridization that seems to happen between species, plus the color variations within species, and I had to throw up my hands in resignation. I really don't know exactly which species of **clouded sulphur butterflies** our Father of details sent to our two acres. I simply named this specimen "clouded yellow sulphur butterfly," although that name actually refers to the genus, not the species.

The *eurytheme* species (very similar to *philodice*), is sometimes called alfalfa butterfly. In large numbers, they can damage alfalfa fields, but otherwise they are a harmless bunch. Their color ranges from yellow to orange-yellow, with a white morph found in females.

Among the row of drab-colored moths of our collection, this clouded yellow sulphur shines like the sun bursting through the clouds. Do you suppose our Father of details likes to brighten our cloudy days with a reminder that He cares about the details of our lives? It seems we humans messed up by naming these sun-splashed butterflies "clouded"!

SPECIES #12

KINGDOM: Animalia
PHYLUM: Arthropoda
CLASS: Insecta
ORDER: Lepidoptera
FAMILY: Pieridae
GENUS: *Colias*
SPECIES: *philodice*

Munching Invaders

Since their accidental introduction to Quebec around 1860, **cabbage white butterflies** have become the most abundant butterfly in North America. Few of our summer safari excursions passed without seeing one of these dancing across the garden. Cabbage whites are the first butterflies to fly in the spring, and they stay active until they freeze in the fall. Other common names include imported cabbage worm, small white, and cabbage butterfly.

Cabbage whites are voracious eaters; even as they brighten the garden, they devour it. The offspring of one female can multiply to millions in a few generations. The larvae go through five instars, eating and eating as they grow. Once they become adults, they live only a few weeks.

When the female is ready to lay eggs, she lands on a host plant and thumps it a couple of times with her forelegs. This gives her the "feel" of the plant—she's looking for a leaf with the consistency of stiff paper—and lets her detect the presence of *glucosinolates*, the "smelly" oils in mustard plants. She will only deposit eggs where glucosinolates are present. She avoids laying her eggs in cloudy or rainy weather when they would be at risk of being washed off the plant. Like many other insects, the larvae in the later instars can go into diapause when the weather chills, thus preserving the species.

Because of their simple color scheme, many people think the cabbage white is a moth. I confess I searched for information about the "cabbage white moth" when I started writing these paragraphs. One difference between moths and butterflies is that butterflies are *diurnal*—active mainly during the day—while moths are *nocturnal*—active at night. Since I had often seen the cabbage white floating along during the day, I should have known it wasn't a moth. As we were initiated into the wonderful world of diversity our Father of details has generously sprinkled on our two acres, we quickly realized how ignorant we were of His bounty!

Detail of a cabbage white wing.

SPECIES #13

KINGDOM: Animalia
PHYLUM: Arthropoda
CLASS: Insecta
ORDER: Lepidoptera
FAMILY: Pieridae
GENUS: *Pieris*
SPECIES: *rapae*

The Contests

I lined up these three caterpillars for two contests. The first is subjective, meaning the results will depend totally upon personal opinion. The second is objective, meaning it deals with facts apart from personal feelings. Contest One is a beauty contest—which of these three is the prettiest? Contest Two is an identification contest—name the moth these caterpillars will become after metamorphosis. When you are ready, turn the page to find the answers.

Answer to moth-naming exercise:
Who doesn't know the ubiquitous woolly worm on the right? But did you guess that this caterpillar turns into an **Isabella tiger moth**? The two caterpillars on the left are both larvae of the **Virginia tiger moth**. That's right, they can be either white or yellow!

Tiger Queen

As a child, I heard a common myth which claimed that the Indians used the woolly bear's band colors to predict the weather—the wider the brown in the middle, the milder the coming winter. It turns out that in 1948, entomologist Howard C. Curran actually conducted an informal study to see if the facts supported the claim. For eight years he collected woolly bear caterpillars in an area north of New York City. The average amount of brown varied from 5.3 to 5.8 of the caterpillar's thirteen bands. However, Curran collected too few specimens from

SPECIES #14

KINGDOM: Animalia
PHYLUM: Arthropoda
CLASS: Insecta
ORDER: Lepidoptera
FAMILY: Arctiidae
GENUS: *Pyrrharctia*
SPECIES: *isabella*

too small an area to draw any conclusions.

Since that time researchers have found that the coloration of woolly worms may be connected to the weather in a different way. The older a specimen gets, the browner it turns. On the other hand, rain can make them blacker. Of course, this is not a prediction of the weather, but it could indicate past weather. A late spring could result in woolly bears emerging later, making them younger and browner the following fall. Likewise, an early chill could send the caterpillars into hibernation younger than usual, again leading to a browner coloration in the hibernating caterpillars. However, a late spring or an early winter do not predict a hard winter.

A special trait of the woolly worms is the ability our Father of details gave them to produce **cryoprotectants**, substances which serve as antifreeze. Since a caterpillar must feed for a few months before it can become a moth, woolly bears in cold regions do not have enough time to reach adulthood in one summer. The cryoprotectants allow them to freeze solid and survive several arctic winters—in one reported case, fourteen winters—until they gain enough sustenance to build a cocoon and turn into an Isabella tiger moth.

Detail of an Isabella tiger moth eye. Each cell is an individual "eye" that works with the others to make up the whole compound eye. The white spot in the middle appears to be a fungus or drop of some substance. This is a dried specimen, so dirt and other objects are on the eye. I assume a living specimen would keep its eyes cleaner.

Check out the neat antennae on this Virginia tiger moth! They are not just an adornment; they are supersensitive pheromone detectors. Insects use chemicals called pheromones to trigger social responses from other members of the same species.

SPECIES #15

KINGDOM: Animalia
PHYLUM: Arthropoda
CLASS: Insecta
ORDER: Lepidoptera
FAMILY: Arctiidae
GENUS: *Spilosoma*
SPECIES: *virginica*

Yellow Woolly Bears

The yellow morph of the Virginia tiger moth caterpillar is more common than the white one shown here. The caterpillar is sometimes called woolly bear, but is usually referred to as a yellow woolly bear. These two caterpillars were within a few feet of each other in our garden, and the banded woolly bear was not too far away, so all three came into our collection together.

The Virginia tiger moth was one of the first specimens we collected. It was the first time I had looked at a moth closely, and those graceful, feathered antennae impressed me. The feathered antennae on certain moth species are so sensitive that the male can "smell" just a couple of pheromone molecules given off by a female miles away.

Unfortunately, I had to dispose of this specimen a couple of weeks later due to a rotting odor. Had I realized earlier that it was beginning to rot, I could have popped it in the freezer to kill the bacteria feeding on it. I have found that freezing caterpillars to euthanize them does not preserve them. Within a couple of days, the hairs fell out of some specimens. (The banded woolly bear has kept his hair as of the time of writing.) Now that the caterpillars are identified, they will have to be discarded.

The simple beauty of these elegant Virginia tiger moths makes them one of my favorites among the oodles of moths we collected during our backyard safari.

My·co·pho·bi·a:
{Fear of fungi}

Meet the fungi, the "employees" of our Father of details' automatic composting system! Did you know the world's largest known living organism is a fungus? Does that sound like the theme of a scary story to entertain children? Well, it isn't; it's a simple fact. The world's largest living organism is a honey fungus *(Armillaria ostoyae)* that stretches across 2,200 acres of land in eastern Oregon. Most of this fungus is underground, consisting of small hair-like fibers called **mycelium**. It is estimated to weigh up to six hundred tons.

When we think of fungi, we often think of mushrooms and mold. However, a mushroom is merely the fruiting body of a larger organism which is often invisible as it feeds on and grows through rotting wood or earth. A mushroom is to a fungus as a flower is to a rose bush.

Fungi are specially designed to break down dead material. Once fungal spores settle into a mass of organic material, they silently go to work, feeding on and breaking down the interior. When the fungus matures, it sprouts a "flower" in the form of a mushroom. Without the mycelium "roots" spreading through the log or other host, the host would lie there for decades or even centuries without rotting and becoming compost on the forest floor. Imagine your favorite woods without any fungi. It would be a tangled mess of dead branches, fallen trees, and leaves from centuries of accumulation! Now are you glad for fungi?

Why do so many people fear fungi? Maybe it's related to why we fear spiders—lack of understanding coupled with a vague sense of danger. Molds can make us sick, and eating the wrong mushroom can send you to the emergency room—or the mortuary. As an old saying warns, "There are *old* mushroom eaters and *bold* mushroom eaters, but there are no *old, bold* mushroom eaters." A healthy respect for the dangers of fungi is appropriate. However, considering all the good they do, most of us need to learn to appreciate them more.

NOT A HAMBURGER BUN!

"Don't eat me! Although some affirm I am safe to eat if you boil me first and throw out the water, you are wiser to just let me be. My immature mushroom has sometimes been mistaken for an edible puffball and made the eaters sick or delirious. Just leave me alone to do my job of turning organic materials into rich compost!"

SPECIES #16

KINGDOM: Fungi
PHYLUM: Basidiomycota
CLASS: Agaricomycetes
ORDER: Agaricales
FAMILY: Amanitaceae
GENUS: *Amanita*
SPECIES: *muscaria*

Are the fungi in this journal edible? The best answer is, "No mushroom is edible unless you are positive it is." If you are starving, experimenting may be in order. Otherwise, stick to eating mushrooms you know to be safe, and enjoy the unique beauty of the others, like this **fly agaric mushroom**.

Admirable Admiral

Male **red admiral butterflies** are territorial, patrolling an area twelve to forty feet wide by twenty-five to seventy feet long. The male makes the rounds of his territory as often as every two minutes, driving away any intruding butterflies. On the other hand, red admirals are known to be people-friendly, occasionally delighting or scaring people by landing on them.

The specimen in our photo is quite ragged, but in this case it was due to more than our sloppy handling; it came into our possession looking worn. Perhaps it was attacked by a predator, escaping with a shredded tail. The missing part is a red band on the rear of the rear wing.

SPECIES #17

KINGDOM: Animalia
PHYLUM: Arthropoda
CLASS: Insecta
ORDER: Lepidoptera
FAMILY: Nymphalidae
GENUS: *Vanessa*
SPECIES: *atalanta*

Habits

Although they will eat other plants, red admiral larvae prefer to eat nettles. The adults drink nectar, so they are often seen on flowering plants, their splash of red adding to the flower's beauty. Red admirals in northern regions are known to migrate south, somewhat as monarchs do, though they are not known to return to specific areas like the monarchs.

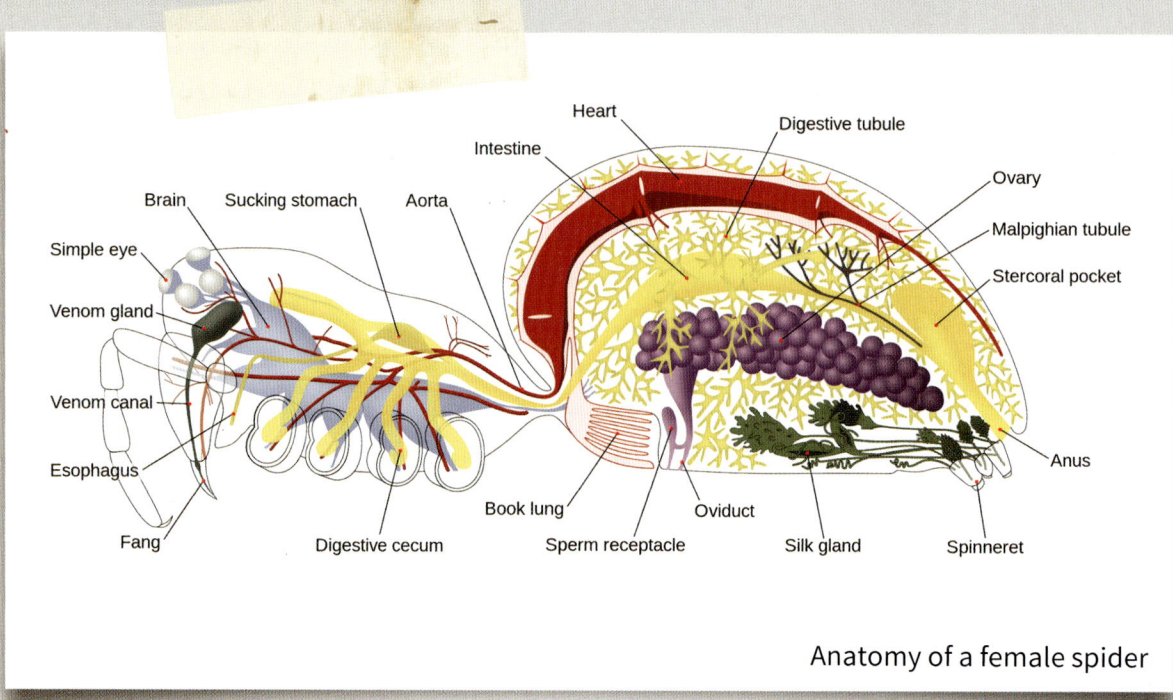

Anatomy of a female spider

Lost on Our Safari!

Only about 3 percent of the 43,000-plus spider species have a common name. Most are known by family names, like wolf spider or jumping spider. Should you decide to go on your own backyard safari, don't feel bad if you cannot assign a species identity to your specimens.

The eye diagrams on the opposite page were a tremendous asset in identifying our spider finds. The diagrams give a representation of the family, so individual species may vary slightly from the diagram. However, the variation is small enough that the diagram should allow you to identify the family. Once you identify the family, you have a better chance of identifying the species.

Still, many times during our safari we were lost in the jungle of species identification. On some of them, we are still not sure if identifications are correct. As you browse through our journal, see if you can identify the spiders by their eye patterns. You may find out how lost we really were—and are!

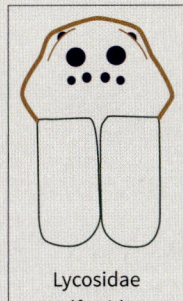
Lycosidae
Wolf spiders

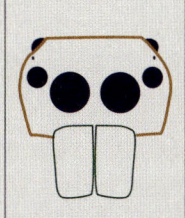
Salticidae
Jumping spiders

Araneidae
Orbweavers

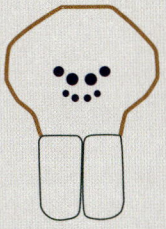
Pisauidae
Fishing spiders

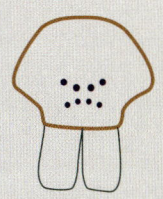
Pisauidae
Nursery web spider

Ctenidae
Wandering spiders

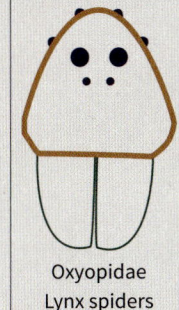
Oxyopidae
Lynx spiders

Philodromidae
Running crab spiders

Dysderidae
Woodlouse hunters

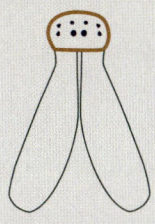
Tetragnathidae
Long-jawed orbweaver

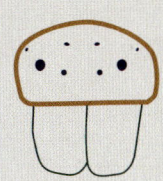
Thomisidae
Ground crab spiders

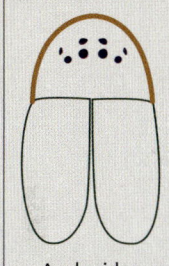
Agelenidae
Funnel weavers

Agelenidae
Grass funnel weaver

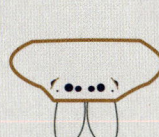
Selenopidae
Crab spiders

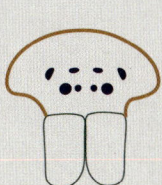
Sparassidae
Huntsman

Sparassidae
Giant crab spiders

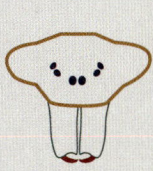
Sicariidae
Brown spiders

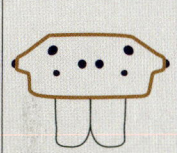
Uloboridae
Triangle weavers

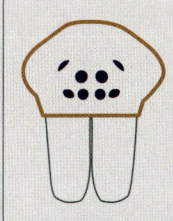
Zoropsidae
False wolf spiders

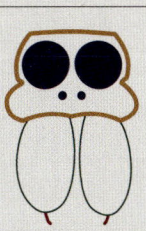
Deinopidae
Ogre-faced spiders

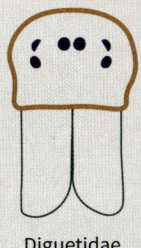
Diguetidae
Desertshrub spiders

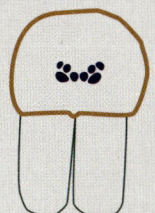
Antrodiaetidae
Folding door spiders

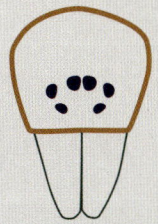
Segestriidae
Tube web spiders

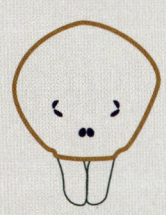
Scytodidae
Spitting spiders

Ornate Exterminators

Long known as the **spiny-bellied orb weaver**, this species has recently gained the common name CD spider due to the way its *iridescent* web shimmers with rainbow colors in sunlight. This name is clearly new, since Compact Discs have only existed for a little over thirty years. The more common name is spined micrathena, and the species name, *gracilis,* is Latin for "graceful" or "slender."

Although arachnophobes might have a hard time thinking of any spider as graceful, when the spined micrathena hangs head down with its shiny white spines protruding, it can resemble a jewel. The spines deceive predators into thinking this sharp object would not make a good munchie; however, the spines are not as hard as they appear.

Like other orb weavers, the spiny orb weaver eats the center part of its web every night and rebuilds it daily. This species is notorious for building webs in forests. If you run into a spider web in the woods, it likely belongs to a spiny orb weaver. The male usually lives near the female, but is smaller and less noticeable. He spins a line up to the female's web and waits for her to mature. Like many other spider species, the male is often eaten by the female.

Drying spiders does not work well. The abdomens shrivel up and deform the specimens, and they lose their color, as you can see in the inset photo on the opposite page. I learned too late that arachnologists preserve specimens in vials of alcohol.

It may sound repetitious, but I will say it again: if you prefer organic pest control for your garden or yard, leave the spiny orb weavers alone. One person has called them "ornate exterminators." Well said! Our Father of details has done a wonderful job in creating these living jewels!

SPECIES #18

KINGDOM: Animalia
PHYLUM: Arthropoda
CLASS: Arachnida
ORDER: Araneae
FAMILY: Araneidae
GENUS: Micrathena
SPECIES: gracilis

Tympanum on this cricket knee is here.

Also, notice that a butterfly scale somehow landed here.

Singing Wings, Hearing Knees

What "sings" with its wings and hears with "ears" just below the knee? Of course you guessed it—you most likely looked at the picture! I knew some insects "sing," or stridulate, by rubbing their wings or legs together, but I didn't know **fall field crickets** had their hearing organs, called tympana, just below their knees.

Our Father of details sometimes seems to have done "weird" things just to reveal His uniqueness, power, and glory. Who would have thought to put a cricket's ears right below its knees? But look at the picture—what is the highest part of a cricket when sitting in a normal position? The knees! By placing them on the highest part of the body, facing forward, God has positioned them for maximum effectiveness. Like humans, crickets can discern the direction of sounds by slight differences in the sound received by each tympanum.

Even more amazing, our Father of details has given crickets the ability to regrow a lost tympanum. In one study, researchers cut one tympanum off various crickets to study how they respond to sound direction. The researchers were astonished to find the amputated tympanum growing back later! The *"creak, creak, creak"* sound they make

SPECIES #19

KINGDOM: Animalia
PHYLUM: Arthropoda
CLASS: Insecta
ORDER: Orthoptera
FAMILY: Gryllidae
GENUS: *Gryllus*
SPECIES: *pennsylvanicus*

FRIED CRICKETS, ANYONE?

earned crickets their English name, which derives from the French noun *criquet*, from the verb *criquer*, "to creak." Each cricket species makes a unique creak. Crickets sing by rubbing a row of tooth-like structures on the underside of one forewing across a ridge on the top side of the other wing, like a comb running across a tight string. One study has found that most crickets are "right-winged," meaning they usually sing by pulling the right wing over the left.

Most cricket chirping is done by males seeking a female. (Two fighting males produce another type of song.) The mating call of some species of crickets can be heard a mile away!

Chirping rate varies by temperature: the warmer the air, the faster the song. Although each species varies a bit, the rate is consistent enough that in 1897 Amos Dolbear created a formula called Dolbear's Law to find the temperature by counting the chirps of a cricket. The simplified version is "Temperature [F] = 40 + Number of chirps in 15 seconds." Count the chirps of a cricket in fifteen seconds and add forty to get the approximate temperature in degrees Fahrenheit!

The cricket on this page has a long **ovipositor** sticking out between the two **cerci** (the shorter appendages on the tail end). This is a female specimen with broken antennae. She pushes the ovipositor (from *ovi*, meaning "egg," and *positor*, meaning "positioner") into the soil to lay her eggs, about fifty at a time, up to four hundred eggs per season. This is the same organ that is modified to serve as a stinger in worker bees and wasps. Apparently our Father of details decided the ovipositor would be more useful to bees and wasps as a defense mechanism.

SPECIES #20

KINGDOM: Animalia
PHYLUM: Arthropoda
CLASS: Insecta
ORDER: Lepidoptera
FAMILY: Sphingidae
GENUS: *Darapsa*
SPECIES: *myron*

Creeper Feeder

Our Father of details has given certain species an instinct to feed on certain plants. Can you guess what plants the **Virginia creeper sphinx moth**, also known as the grapevine sphinx, prefers? Virginia creeper (below) and grapevines, of course! Also known as the hog sphinx—from its appearance, I assume—this species also feeds on other plants when its favorites are not available. The caterpillars of this moth are often bright green, with a peculiar "horn" sticking out at the tail end. Through its five instars, the colors and shapes of the caterpillar and horn change, with the horn growing progressively shorter.

SPECIES #21

KINGDOM: Animalia
PHYLUM: Arthropoda
CLASS: Arachnida
ORDER: Araneae
FAMILY: Lycosidae
GENUS: *Tigrosa?*
SPECIES: *aspersa?*

Wandering Wolves

This family of spiders earned the Greek family name *lukos*—**wolf spiders**—for their hunting style. Instead of building a web and waiting for prey to come to them, they wander around like a wolf, looking for something to catch. Although they usually snatch their prey in a simple surprise attack, they have also been known to chase down prey.

With more than a hundred genera (13 in the U.S.) and 2,300 species (250 in the U.S.) worldwide—well, I tried to identify the exact species for these specimens, but I simply got lost. I have tentatively identified the pictured specimens as *Tigrosa aspersa*. (To further complicate matters, *aspersa* was moved from the *Hogna* genus to *Tigrosa* in 2012. This is an example of the unsettled nature of the taxonomy of spiders and insects.)

Some wolf spiders live in a burrow, while others tend to wander without a fixed home. With their reflective eyes and their habit of nocturnal hunting, these are likely the owners of the tiny eyes you might see twinkling in the grass if you shine a flashlight on the lawn at night. Wolf spiders can and do bite humans, but only when provoked by handling. They are venomous, but the bite is typically no worse than a bee sting, if that. From my research, it appears that no one has ever died from a wolf spider bite.

Wolf spiders are some of the best spider mothers. The female makes a silk egg case and attaches it to her spinnerets, hauling the eggs with her until they hatch, as seen on pages 76–77.[1] For weeks after they hatch, the young often hitch a ride on the mother's back. The Carolina wolf spider has the distinction of being the only official state spider in the United States. South Carolina chose it in 2000, probably with a bit of bias in favor of its name.

---

[1] This specimen did not come from our two acres, but from a neighboring property. It is included here because we *do* have many wolf spiders on our two acres, and this specimen is too fine an example of a female towing her eggs to leave out of our journal. This is also one of the few spider specimens we dried that ended up turning out well.

Can Spiders Re-Grow Lost Legs?

Yes and no. Growing spiders go through several instars. When the *exoskeleton* gets too small for the expanding interior soft parts, the spider will essentially step out of its old shell, and a larger, harder one will quickly form on the new instar. When a spider gets a new skeleton, it gets new legs, since the legs have few soft parts and are almost totally replaced. If it loses a leg or two to a predator, after the next instar it will again have all eight legs.

However, if a spider loses some legs after it has finished its last instar, it can never replace those legs. This wolf spider (above) has lost some legs. It is easy to see how they can be pulled right out of their little sockets. Having a leg that detaches easily is a defense mechanism. If a predator grabs a leg, the spider can simply let the predator keep the leg and go on with life. An immature spider will soon get all new legs anyway.

Not Spiders!

I admit I called "granddaddy longlegs" spiders all my life—until I studied them for this book. One is never too old to learn, especially on a backyard safari! These are **harvestmen**. Like spiders, they are arachnids, but they are in a separate order from spiders.

What differentiates harvestmen from spiders? Spiders have two body segments, while harvestmen have only one. I suppose you could call them "no-neckers." Also, instead of six or eight eyes like spiders, harvestmen have two, on a little turret near the front of their body. Next time you see a granddaddy longlegs, look carefully to see if it is a harvestman or a spider!

Like spiders, harvestmen have eight legs with seven segments. If we humans had legs in equal proportions to harvestmen, ours would be forty feet long! Harvestmen have been called shepherd spiders because of their likeness to shepherds in parts of Europe who used to walk on stilts while herding their flocks. Those long legs serve more purposes than walking—the second pair is equipped with very sensitive feelers on the tips. Harvestmen can also walk on water.

Granddaddy longlegs are the victims

SPECIES #22

KINGDOM: Animalia
PHYLUM: Arthropoda
CLASS: Arachnida
ORDER: Opiliones
FAMILY:
GENUS:
SPECIES:

of strange rumors. One story claims they are the most poisonous spiders, but that their mouth is too small to bite humans. This is wrong in two important ways: first, harvestmen are not spiders, and second, harvestmen do not have venom. However, harvestmen do "make a stink" as a defense mechanism when threatened.

More than 6,500 species of harvestmen have been named worldwide, and some specialists estimate that there are probably more than 10,000 species in all. Now you know why the family, genus, and species blocks are empty on the species card. Harvestmen are an understudied order with some really unique and interesting species, including a bright lime green species and some colorful horned species in Brazil.

The one specimen I dried turned out well. It was probably close to four inches in diameter (leg length, of course). When the time came to photograph it, I carefully pulled on the mounting pin to see if the body had stuck to it, as it tends to do. It moved freely! I was feeling triumphant—I had a trophy. I pulled the pin some more, with my fingers against the body. I don't know how it happened, but there was a light crunching sound, and most of the legs instantly fell off. Our safari has had some hard learning curves. The top right photo shows the details of a harvestman's jaws. The opposite page shows a head.

Thin Head

The real English common name for this mushroom is **nitrous bonnet**, but "thin head" is the translation of the Greek species name. As with insects and spiders, too many similar species exist for me to make a definite identification of this fungus. The Mycenaceae family has 705 species.

The name *nitrous bonnet* comes from the odor emitted by this and similar species. Some say it smells like bleach. It grows in many parts of the world, including our two acres. The intricacy of this creation of our Father of details intrigues me. The photos do not do them justice. How privileged we are to have them here!

SPECIES #23

KINGDOM: Fungi
PHYLUM: Basidiomycota
CLASS: Basidiomycetes
ORDER: Agaricales
FAMILY: Mycenaceae
GENUS: *Mycena*
SPECIES: *leptocephala*

Slug Bug

Don't ask me how we came to call them slug bugs. No, I don't mean the ubiquitous **ladybird beetle**, but the Volkswagen Beetle. My childhood was full of watching out for "slug bugs" and trying to win the game by being the first to holler, "Slug bug!" and slug a sibling when one was spotted.

Our Father of details designed the ladybird beetle, or ladybug, but the driving force behind the design of the Volkswagen Beetle was none other than Adolf Hitler. His quest to develop a simple and affordable vehicle for the common people (*volken* in German) led to the production of the VW Beetle.

In its early days, the vehicle was called the Volkswagen Type 1, but who could miss the similarity to a ladybird beetle? The *volken* of Germany dubbed it *Käfer* (beetle) and the name stuck. Soon the vehicle was marketed worldwide as the Volkswagen Beetle. It

SPECIES #24

KINGDOM: Animalia
PHYLUM: Arthropoda
CLASS: Insecta
ORDER: Coleoptera
FAMILY: Coccinellidae
GENUS:
SPECIES:

ended up being the most produced vehicle style in the history of the automobile industry, with over 21,000,000 Beetles puttering around the globe over a 66-year span.

As economic and functional as the VW Beetle was, have you ever pondered how many times more amazing is the ladybird beetle created by our Father of details? Shrink the VW model down to one-thousandth of its size. Add a propulsion system that takes in insects and plant material, digests them to draw out the fuel, and automatically refills the tank when needed. Throw in some eyes that capture certain frequencies of radiation and turn it into what we call sight. Add some wings so it can take off flying when it feels like it; and of course legs are standard equipment for terrestrial purposes. Don't forget about its ability to propagate itself with no factories required. Yet people marvel over the VW version more than over the living and breathing beetle!

Did you notice that there is no genus or species name for these photos? There are more than 5,000 species of ladybird beetles, including 450 in the United States. And I always thought a ladybug was a ladybug. A quick look at a ladybug identification key informed me that for species identification I need to know several details:

1. The number of spots on the abdomen
2. The color of the abdomen
3. The pattern on the abdomen (spots, stripes, solid, banded, or mottled)
4. The pattern on the **pronotum**, the front upper part of the thorax (spotted, solid, or complex)
5. The main color of the pronotum
6. The number of spots, if any, on the pronotum

I simply felt too overwhelmed to try to identify the exact species in these photos. By the way, it is a myth that a ladybug's age can be determined by the number of spots it has.

Ladybugs are commonly seen gathering in the fall as they seek shelter from the coming winter. Dismantling an old house trailer this year, we encountered hundreds, maybe thousands, of specimens in the walls and ceilings. Some dried beetles appeared to have been there for a long time already. Knowing the ladybugs' appetite for aphids, most gardeners have a positive view of them. However, in some neighborhoods they have made a nuisance of themselves, causing more problems than they solved. As even the Bible indicates in Proverbs 25:16, too much of a good thing yields undesirable results.

Daniel took this picture the fall before our safari began, but it was from our two acres. How many species of ladybird beetles, or ladybugs, do you see here? Remember, coloration can vary within species.

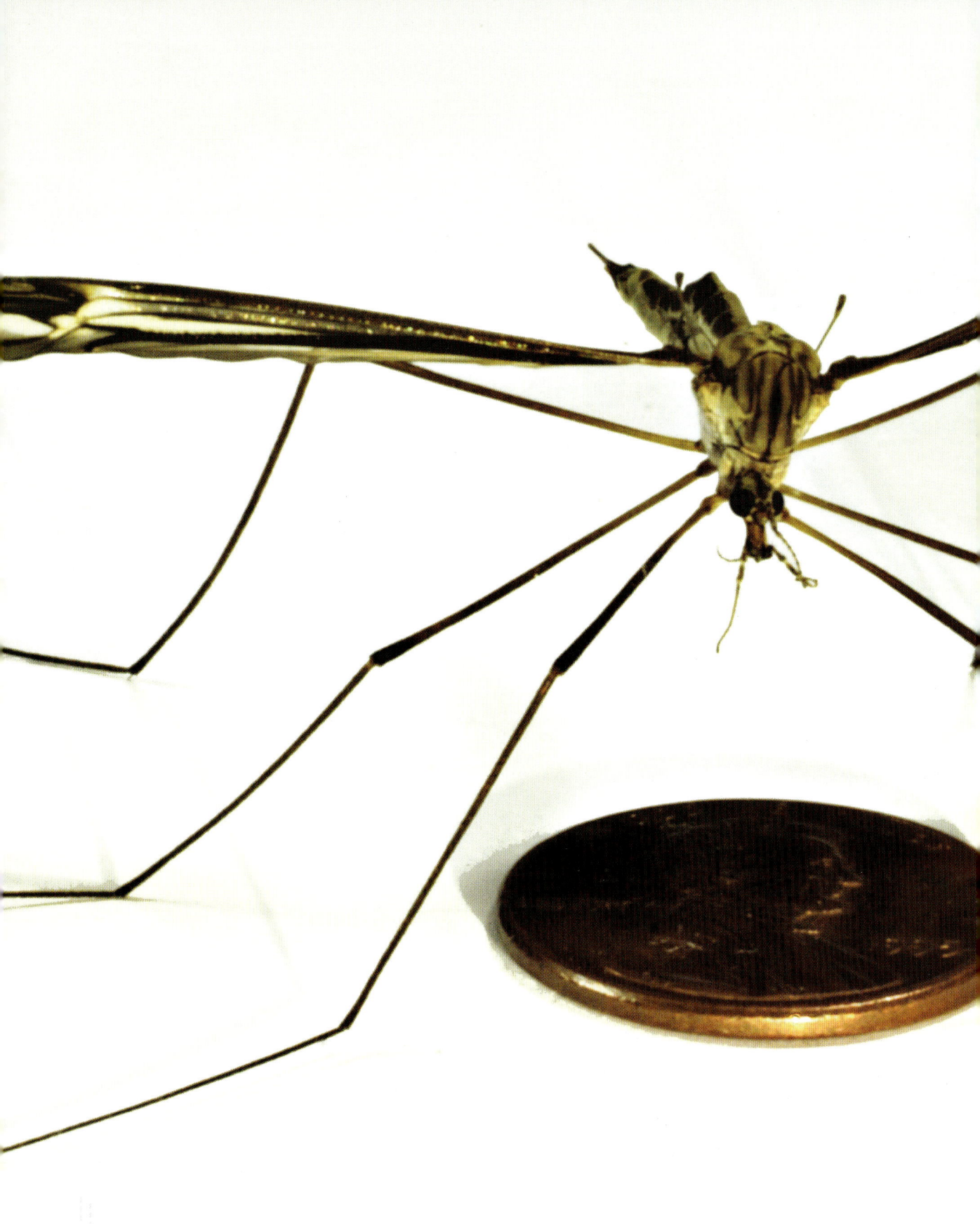

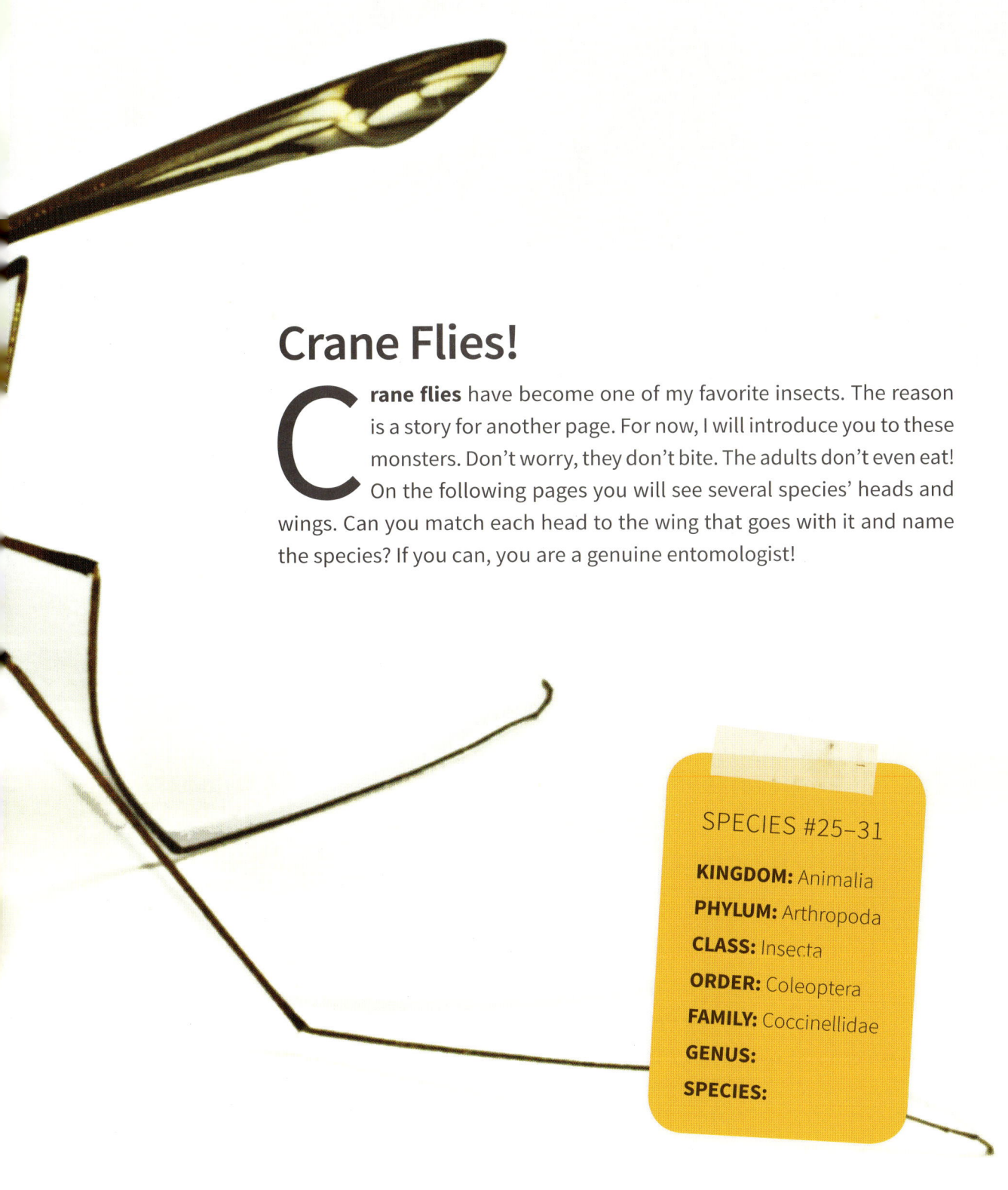

Crane Flies!

Crane flies have become one of my favorite insects. The reason is a story for another page. For now, I will introduce you to these monsters. Don't worry, they don't bite. The adults don't even eat! On the following pages you will see several species' heads and wings. Can you match each head to the wing that goes with it and name the species? If you can, you are a genuine entomologist!

SPECIES #25–31

KINGDOM: Animalia
PHYLUM: Arthropoda
CLASS: Insecta
ORDER: Coleoptera
FAMILY: Coccinellidae
GENUS:
SPECIES:

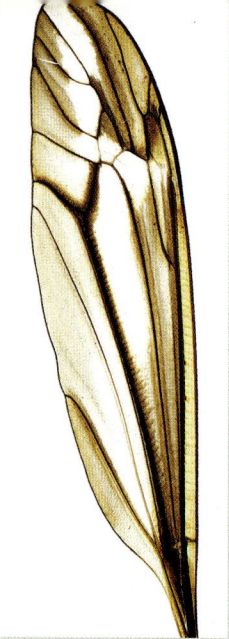

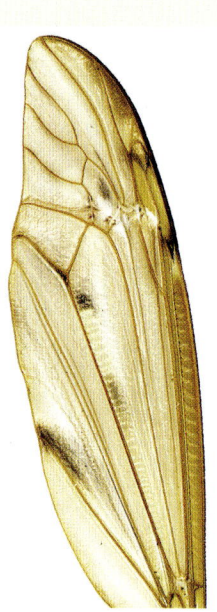

Head Match

On this page are seven heads and seven wings. Match the correct head to the correct wing and then give the correct species name. The answers are on page 92. Here are the species names:

1. *Pedicia albivitta*
2. *Tipula nobilis*
3. *Tipula caloptera*
4. *Tipula furca*
5. *Tipula tricolor*
6. *Nephrotoma virescens*
7. *Epiphragma solatrix*

Note the differences in the vein patterns on the wings. Some are very slight, like the difference between the third and fourth wings from the left. On the heads, count the antennae segments, check the color of the segments, and pay attention to the nose length and the form of the palps. These specimens are all from our two-acre lot. And to think that before our safari began, I didn't even know what a crane fly was!

"Who is like unto thee, O LORD, among the gods? who is like thee, glorious in holiness, fearful in praises, doing wonders?" (Exodus 15:11).

Answers

I made it really easy for you. The heads and the wings are matched vertically and arranged from left to right according to their numbers in the species list. If you tried to do the exercise, you now have a better sense of the challenge of species identification.

Crane Fly Craze

As I mentioned earlier, crane flies have gained a special place in my heart. It all began with a phone call to Anthony Hurst, formerly of Myerstown, Pennsylvania. Anthony is a veritable entomologist, not a wannabe like me. About two years ago I was at Myerstown Mennonite School, where Anthony taught, and I saw his insect collection—a thousand strong. At the time, insects were just a passing interest to me. Later, when the idea for this journal was in the early stages, we remembered Anthony's collection, and I found his telephone number.

While talking to Anthony about the journal idea, I happened to notice a huge "bug" on the inside of the window screen. I had no idea what it was, and I mentioned it to Anthony. As I gave him a brief description, he mentioned a name, but it didn't stick. Ending the call, I decided this insect might make a nice specimen for the proposed project. The journal was still only a dream, but for dreams to become reality, sometimes we have to take the first step. We rose to the challenge and captured the "bug," which wasn't hard—crane flies are not aggressive.

What to do with the captured insect? I really didn't know. Anthony had mentioned that although some people gas their specimens, he prefers to freeze them. A quick call back to him confirmed that we should probably pop it in the freezer for about fifteen minutes. Somehow I quickly learned that this "bug" was a crane fly. Identification of the exact species didn't come so easily. In fact, it was several months later until I think I finally got it right.

An hour or so after that first catch and freeze, we found another crane fly, this time on the window screen of the bathroom. Yes, this one was inside the house too; the basement door is opposite the bathroom door and doesn't always get latched properly. Soon Daniel brought another huge specimen up from the basement. Crane flies love damp places, and most likely these were hatching from eggs laid by a crane fly that had found its way into the basement the previous season.

On photographing the specimen from the bathroom, I noticed that it had three ocelli, or eye spots, between the two big eyes. This was a different species than the others! Not until months later would I notice that this bathroom specimen had two sets of wings, rather than two wings with **halteres** (see page 95). It wasn't even a crane fly at all! For a couple of weeks, now that we had a name for these insects and were watching for small creations of our Father of details, it seemed we saw crane flies everywhere.

We collected a few, tried to dry them, and learned that crane flies are notorious for losing legs. In a later conversation, Anthony laughingly commented that he has "glued a lot of legs on." I tried using super glue—a good lesson in patience!

July came, and crane flies were nowhere to be found. With our motley collection of partially legged specimens, I was beginning to wonder if we would be able to get any more full-legged specimens to photograph. Then at the end of August, crane flies were suddenly everywhere again. Evidently they have two hatches per year in our area. Noticing a few different wing patterns, I began to add more to the collection. The day came to sort them. I thought I might have three or four species, but we identified seven species, not counting the phantom crane fly! Also, there in the pile was another specimen with two sets of wings—not a crane fly.

I suppose my liking for crane flies is connected to that first excitement of catching and identifying an unknown species. Whatever it is, I confess that crane flies have become special to me. They are neat little creatures!

In this photo you can see our motley crowd of crane flies, some pinned and some lying amidst the array of broken legs. The basic principle of drying insects is simple: put a pin through the thorax and position the legs in the position where you want them to dry. However, this is easier said than done! Crane fly legs fall off with the slightest bump. I don't think we succeeded in keeping all the legs intact on any of our crane fly specimens.

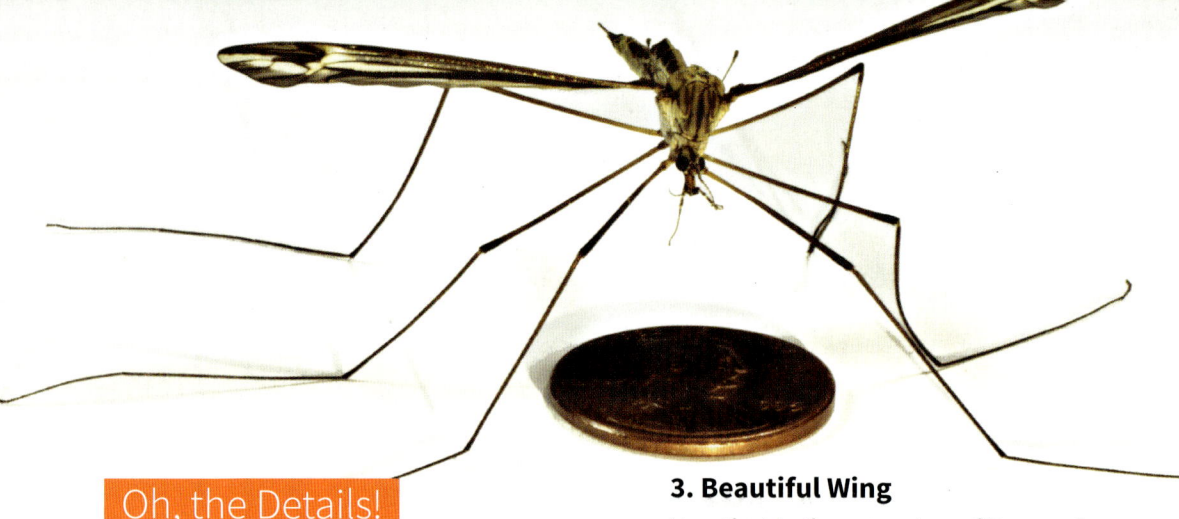

Oh, the Details!

Here are a few details about several of those seven crane fly species on page 90.

1. Big Crane

The great eastern crane fly is one of the few crane flies with a common name. Its name comes from its relatively large size and its range, which is in the eastern United States. The species name *albivitta* is Latin for white (*albi*) striped (*vitta*). This probably refers to the white stripes on its lower abdomen, although some specimens also have whitish wings. With a leg span of almost four inches across, these are impressive crane flies. If they bit like mosquitos relative to their size, they would have a whammer of a bite! However, crane flies are harmless to humans, although a few species have been known to cause damage to plants.

2. Noble Fellow

The Latin species name of this crane fly, *nobilis,* means "noble" or "notable," but it has no common name, and there is nothing particularly striking about it. To most of us, it's just another crane fly. Yet our Father of details designed this species, like every other, for a reason.

3. Beautiful Wing

Yes, that is the meaning of its species name, *caloptera*. This fly is simple, yet elegant. The wing of *T. furca* is very similar to that of *T. caloptera*, but a closer look reveals a clear difference in color.

6. Green Crane

Virescens translates as "becoming green." This crane fly species has a wing very similar to the *Tipula* genus, but some specimens have a vivid greenish or yellow body color. The specimen pictured has already faded. I learned too late that once a specimen starts to dry, it often loses some or all of its brilliant colors. Some people call this a tiger crane fly, but that is actually the common name of the genus *Nephrotoma,* which includes more than forty species in North America.

7. Not Lemonade, *Limoniidae*

The wing design of this little crane fly immediately sets it apart from the others. It is from the Limoniidae family rather than the Coccinellidae family. Crane flies in the Limoniidae family hold their wings straight back when resting, while other crane fly families hold the wings out at ninety degrees. Had I known this detail when drying this specimen, I would have positioned the wings properly.

Halteres

Yes, the word is spelled right. They are not halters, they are halteres, although the singular form is halter. The photo above is a pair of crane fly halteres. The word comes from the Greek word *alter,* or halter (from the verb *allomai*, "to jump"), and refers to a pair of handheld weights used by ancient Greek athletes to improve their performance in the long jump by swinging them forward at launch and backward at landing.

In flies, mosquitos, and gnats, the halteres replace the rear wings found on most insects. These beat up and down rapidly, out of sync with the front wings, creating a gyroscopic "sensor" that can register minute changes in body position and stabilize the flight. A housefly typically beats its wings about two hundred beats per second and can make a ninety-degree turn in about three hundredths of a second! The halteres are heavily involved in this process, both notifying the brain of the body position and counteracting the wings to stop the turn at just the right angle. No wonder they are so hard to swat! Imagine our Father of details creating a built-in gyroscope for insects!

Recent research has found that fly muscles do not even receive an impulse from the brain for every beat, solving the long-standing puzzle of how the muscles could oscillate so rapidly. The researchers found that when one set of wing muscles contracts, it sends a signal to the opposite set; when the other set contracts, it sends a signal back to the first. The brain, instead of sending signals for each wingbeat, simply starts this automatic feedback cycle, guides the turning muscles while the fly is in motion, and turns the cycle off when it's time to stop flying. Ingenious, isn't it?

● One last crane fly detail: an eye. Don't ask me what species it is!

SPECIES #32

KINGDOM: Animalia
PHYLUM: Arthropoda
CLASS: Insecta
ORDER: Lepidoptera
FAMILY: Noctuidae
GENUS: *Noctua*
SPECIES: *pronuba*

Multiplying Moths

Like many moths, the **large yellow underwing** is "bright in flight; bland on land." If a predator sees its yellow wings flashing in flight and approaches, the moth can land on a woody surface and camouflage itself instantly. At rest, its wings fold over its body like a tent.

This moth is a prime example of how quickly moths can multiply. In 1979 it was accidentally introduced to Nova Scotia from Europe. By 1985 it had invaded Maine. It was found in North Carolina in 1997, Colorado in 1999, California in 2001, and Alaska in 2005—twenty-six years to populate a whole continent! At that rate this moth could populate the entire globe in just seventy-five years.

As I pondered this rapid rate of expansion, my mind went to the story of Noah's ark. For some people, the idea that all the animal species in the world were crammed into the ark seems like a fairy tale. How could so many species have fit into one large ship, and how could they have spread over the entire earth so quickly after leaving that ship?

The spread of the large yellow underwing shows that even by natural spreading a species can cover the earth very quickly. But were all the animal species on the earth today inside the ark? There are more than 11,500 moth species fluttering in North America alone!

Obviously, God has set in order what is called *speciation*, the formation of new species. Within the genetic code of each genus lies the possibility for who knows how many more species than exist today. For example, it is assumed that domestic dogs have descended from the gray wolf or a similar species. Today there are approximately 340 breeds of dogs, from tiny chihuahuas to monstrous St. Bernards, and most of these have been developed within the last two hundred years.

If within two or three centuries man can, by selective breeding, develop hundreds of variations in dogs, why couldn't God do the same with all the diverse species that were on the ark with Noah? From one moth species on the ark, God could easily have made tens of thousands of variations and spread them over the earth.

SPECIES #33

KINGDOM: Animalia
PHYLUM: Arthropoda
CLASS: Insecta
ORDER: Coleoptera
FAMILY: Staphylinidae
GENUS: *Platydracus*
SPECIES: *maculosus*

Brown Mystery

This **brown rove beetle** (previous page) showed up one day crawling up our front screen door. I noticed it as I was leaving the house, immediately put my departure on hold, and went for the peanut butter jar to capture it. I could not remember ever having seen such a creature before. It even occurred to me, although not too seriously, that perhaps I had just found a new insect species. Beyond the class, Insecta, I was totally stumped as to its identification.

With some outside help, I finally identified it as *Platydracus* (flat/broad dragon) *maculosus* (spotted), one of the more common rove beetles in our area. I learned that rove beetles are the largest beetle family, with over 58,000 named species and 400 new ones described every year. Some entomologists estimate that about 75 percent of the tropical species have never been described. Rove beetles benefit gardeners by feeding on harmful insects. And to think I do not remember ever hearing of a rove beetle before!

Rove beetles have wings, but the *elytra*—the hard, outer wings—are short, leaving a good part of their abdomen exposed. I thought at first that this specimen was wingless. Looking closely at the beetle pictured, you can see that the elytra end at the rear leg. Notice also the eleven segments on the antennae. Rove beetles always have eleven segments; count them!

The Little Moths

I confess I gave up trying to identify these **micromoths**. Three in our collection are very much alike in shape and color, but I can see enough distinction to surmise that they are three unique species. I also confess that early on in our safari I quit collecting small moths unless they struck me as unique. We simply had enough specimens to fill the journal, and the little creatures are hard to pin and dry. The pins are as large in diameter as the bodies of the smallest ones. (Note the pinhole in the blue paper for a size reference.)

Micromoths are the most understudied group among the moths, probably due to their small size.

SPECIES #34–40

KINGDOM: Animalia
PHYLUM: Arthropoda
CLASS: Insecta
ORDER: Lepidoptera
FAMILY:
GENUS:
SPECIES:

Preying Mantis

Aha! You thought I misspelled the common name, didn't you? I did and I didn't. Most people call them praying mantises, but some do call them preying mantises, a type of mistake that has recently been termed an eggcorn.[1] Regardless, praying mantises do prey; in fact, they are known for eating almost all the time. I always thought there was just one species of praying mantis, but I learned that about twenty distinct praying mantis species inhabit the United States, with about fifteen hundred species worldwide.

Praying mantises gobble down nearly any kind of insect up to their own size, and they have been known to take on even bigger things, including small reptiles and hummingbirds. They "pray" by holding their front legs in a posture that resembles folded hands, but as soon as dinner gets within reach, they *prey* by snapping out forelegs studded with spines to clutch their victims. They are fast; their front legs can snap forward twice before a fly can take off! Praying mantises eat and eat and eat.

Newly hatched praying mantises eat each other, especially if no other food is immediately available. After going through several molts, the young mantises emerge as adults with wings. A male seeking a mate must be extremely careful—many praying mantis females eat males. Some males survive the encounter with a female, but others are eaten even before they have a chance to become a father, or they have their heads bitten off during or immediately after mating, with the rest of the body saved for later.

Do you understand now why I titled this species *preying* mantis? This preying nature has earned the praying mantis a reputation as an asset to gardens. However, while a praying mantis does eat a lot of "bad" insects, it also snatches beneficial insects. Anything it can catch is on the menu.

Mantises are known for their ability to turn their heads 180 degrees, creating some remarkable poses. Their tympanum is located on their underside. An interesting characteristic of a praying mantis "ear" is

---

1   A mistaken substitution of a word that sounds like the correct one without making nonsense of the phrase, such as saying *eggcorn* for *acorn*.

SPECIES #41

KINGDOM: Animalia
PHYLUM: Arthropoda
CLASS: Insecta
ORDER: Mantodea
FAMILY: Polyspilotini
GENUS: *Tenodera*
SPECIES: *sinensis*

that it is tuned to ultrasonic sounds. Why would mantises, that rarely make sounds themselves, need to hear ultrasonic frequencies? Bats! Male mantises fly mostly at night, and a flying mantis makes a good bat meal. When a mantis hears the ultrasonic squeaks of a bat, it can "hit the floor" and try to hide in the grass.

I would normally edit out mediocre photos like the ones on these pages, but when I tried to photograph this specimen in a bush near the house (on two different days), the light was low and I was too lazy to go inside to get a tripod. These slightly blurred photos are the result of my slothfulness. My wife was pretty adamant that I not catch this mantis—its reputation for being beneficial saved its life! When I went for the third photo shoot, it was nowhere to be found. My identification of this specimen as the **Chinese mantis** is based on the stripes on its head. Turn the page now to see the "official" praying mantis.

Irreligious Mantis

With a species name like *religiosa*, one would get the idea that a **praying mantis** is kind and merciful. Make no mistake. The name *religiosa* does not fit this insect's propensity for ravenously eating whatever comes within reach.

This specimen was photographed the year before we officially began our safari. It has striking color and form, with a large gut hanging down, doubtless from eating all the time. Think of all that food going down that narrow throat! Though the image is not extremely clear, you can see the spines on its front legs, which help hold prey. The *Mantis religiosa* was introduced to North America in 1899 on a shipment of nursery plants from Europe, and it has now spread across the continent to the Pacific Ocean. Connecticut has even declared it the official state insect.

SPECIES #42

KINGDOM: Animalia
PHYLUM: Arthropoda
CLASS: Insecta
ORDER: Mantodea
FAMILY: Mantidae
GENUS: *Mantis*
SPECIES: *religiosa*

The One That Got Away

If you have any deer-hunting friends, you have likely heard the story about the big buck with the amazing rack that somehow escaped without a trace. The story of this **mayfly** (previous page) is a little like that.

We did not actually spend much time collecting our specimens for this book. At the beginning of our safari, we would head outdoors and within about fifteen minutes we would have enough specimens to fill our collection jars. Collecting our one hundred-plus specimens probably took a total of four to six hours.

Occasionally Daniel or I headed out with the camera to see if we could catch a shot "in the wild," since the specimens look better in their natural settings. Wandering among the plants in the garden on one of my photo excursions, I encountered this mayfly. I felt just like a deer hunter when a big buck comes into view. I had to get this one! I had never seen anything like it, and I had no idea what it was, but I knew I wanted it in our collection. I wanted to capture it, but I was afraid it would disappear if I ran to the house for a jar. So, I tried to photograph it "native."

The specimen cooperated with me and sat very still as my camera lens approached within inches of its body. I managed to get a couple of nice photos, which is not so easy to do in the wild. My subject remained calm, its haunting red eyes watching me warily.

I still wanted this rare insect for our collection so I could get macro photos for this journal. Should I run for the house and hope it stayed put until I returned with a jar? What if it escaped and I never saw one again? I decided to try to nab it by the wings. I inched my fingers closer, then grabbed for him. I felt the wings between my fingertips, but he got away. My bright red trophy was gone, leaving me with only a story.

Several facts make the mayflies stand out as examples of the ingenuity of our Father of details. First, mayflies have no functional mouthparts, so how do they eat? As adults, they *don't* eat, since adult mayflies live only four to six days. That's the reason for their Greek order name, Ephemeroptera—it means "upon a day," acknowledging that mayflies count their lifespans in days rather than in weeks, months, or years. One species of mayfly has an adult life span of only an hour and a half! Why give a mayfly a mouth if it doesn't need one?

Mayfly nymphs generally live for many months, some as long as two years, feeding on decaying plant material on the bottoms of lakes, ponds, and streams. When the time is right, they come out of the water and molt into a **subimago** (an adult, but without full wings) and then molt again within minutes into an *imago* (adult) to spend their remaining days or hours in search of a mate. After mating, the female lays her eggs in the water, sometimes while in flight.

Mayflies are an important food for fish. Fly fishermen tie some of their flies to imitate mayflies, so if you find a mayfly and want it identified, your local trout angler may be a good source of information.

From mid-May through July along the shores of Lake Erie, about two hours' drive north of our place, the emerging mayflies become a nuisance, swarming in millions around streetlights and yard lights, their dead bodies falling to the ground in a crunchy mess that reeks of dead fish. People clear them off their porches and sidewalks with leaf blowers and shovels, and sometimes snowplows are used to clean them from the streets. The abundance of mayflies is one reason Lake Erie supports as many fish as all the other Great Lakes combined.

Although the eye on my specimen appears to look straight up, its compound eye curves below as well. The black dot on top, which is not a pupil, gives this species an eerie look, like a huge eye focused on your every move.

SPECIES #43

KINGDOM: Animalia
PHYLUM: Arthropoda
CLASS: Insecta
ORDER: Ephemeroptera
FAMILY: Isonychiidae
GENUS: *Isonychia*
SPECIES: *rufa*

Harnessed Tiger

This medium-sized **harnessed tiger moth** has nice colors and markings, but I could find little information about it. Several species of the genus *Apantesis* are so similar in appearance that the only way to be sure is to dissect the specimen. For our purposes, I didn't feel the need to be that particular.

As another example of our learning experience, soon after we finished photographing this specimen, it lost its abdomen, one antenna, and a couple of legs.

SPECIES #44

KINGDOM: Animalia
PHYLUM: Arthropoda
CLASS: Insecta
ORDER: Lepidoptera
FAMILY: Arctiidae
GENUS: *Apantesis*
SPECIES: *phalerata*

SPECIES #45

KINGDOM: Fungi
PHYLUM: Basidiomycota
CLASS: Ustilaginomycetes
ORDER: Ustilaginales
FAMILY: Ustilaginaceae
GENUS: Ustilago
SPECIES: maydis

Quesadilla with truffles. Look good? It supposedly has more protein than corn!

Mexican Truffles

I remember picking sweet corn as a boy and coming across this grotesque-looking growth sprouting out of our sweet corn ears. I was afraid even to touch it for fear of getting some sort of infection. Decades later, I learned that it is a delicacy in Mexico. Mexican farmers sometimes spread the spores in their fields intentionally for extra profit, and the USDA has recently allowed some U.S. farmers to infect their corn with smut as a step toward getting U.S. consumers hooked on eating it.

Corn smut has more protein than the corn plant it infests! The taste is comparable to mushrooms—a mild, earthy flavor. If you happen on a restaurant offering "Mexican truffles," be aware that this is a more palatable name for corn smut.

Unless you plan to add some corn smut into your next batch of tacos, you are better off eradicating it from your corn patch, since it saps the strength of corn plants and reduces yields.

Peanut Wings

I was unloading firewood from the truck one midsummer day when I noticed this striking **net-wing beetle** on the woodpile. At the time, I didn't realize it was in the beetle family; when I think of beetles, I think of crawly, black, ugly things. It was a new find, so I dropped my firewood task and captured it.

When I finally identified this specimen months later, I found that the genus name, *Calopteron,* means "beautiful wing"! The species name, *terminale,* indicates that the black band is on the terminal of the wing; hence the common name of end band net-wing beetle.[1]

Since net-wing beetles taste bad and can even poison small predators, they have few natural enemies. Adults feed mostly on decaying plant matter, while larvae feed on mites and small bugs under tree bark.

---

[1] Two very similar species have another black band midway up the wing (the end band net-wing can also have a middle band, but it is usually narrower in *terminale* than in the other species).

SPIRITUAL LESSON

The net-wing beetle's bad taste and toxic makeup encourage predators to leave him alone. What about the times *we* feel left alone or rejected? Could it be that when others get near us, we give them a bitter mouthful of gossip, ridicule, or scorn? Maybe we, like the net-wing beetles, emit a "bad taste" to defend ourselves; but are harsh words ever appropriate? May we leave the sweet taste of humility, meekness, and love in the mouths of all who encounter us!

SPECIES #46

KINGDOM: Animalia
PHYLUM: Arthropoda
CLASS: Insecta
ORDER: Coleoptera
FAMILY: Lycidae
GENUS: Calopteron
SPECIES: terminale

Notice the live specimen's green eyes in contrast to the color of the same dried specimen's eyes in the inset photo. Dead things can never truly reflect life!

SPECIES #47

KINGDOM: Animalia
PHYLUM: Arthropoda
CLASS: Insecta
ORDER: Lepidoptera
FAMILY: Homorthodes
GENUS: *Homorthodes*
SPECIES: *lindseyi*

In Plain Hiding

The **southern scurfy Quaker moth**, like the early Quakers, is a plain little fellow. However, I am not entirely sure this is indeed a southern scurfy Quaker moth. One reference mentions that the southern scurfy Quaker moth used to be considered a subspecies of the northern scurfy Quaker moth, but is now classified as a separate species.

This specimen happens to match the carpet on our living room floor, where I found him. The amazingly effective camouflage of many animals speaks to the wisdom of our Father of details. Some moth caterpillars look like bird droppings, fooling hungry predators, while some butterflies and moths sport fake eyes to make them appear large and menacing.

Not only are these animals created with the perfect coloration to hide or deter predators, but many of them also seem to be programmed with instinctive behaviors to choose the best resting place and posture to exploit their special camouflage or pattern. All this is overwhelming evidence of design by our Father of details.

Seeing this camouflaged moth, my mind went to evolutionary theory and things I have read concerning how animals developed certain body parts or functions. While official evolutionary theory does not promote the idea that animals have any choice in their ongoing development, you may well see such ideas hinted at in your local advertising paper, or even in "respected" science publications.

For example, in a *National Geographic* article about how human diet supposedly evolved, one scientist wrote: "When humans switched to meat-eating, they triggered a genetic change that enabled better processing of fats."[1] Let's be straightforward here. Could humans really have done something to change their genetics to process fats better? Of course not! Any change in the genetic code to better process fats would have been random change, an accident. Why, then, do evolutionists make such statements?

I surmise that the reason they make such statements is because it sounds more acceptable to credit something other than mere chance for positive changes in a genetic code. Had the author written that "an accidental change in the genetic code happened to produce better fat-processing ability at the exact time when humans began to eat more meat," most people would probably think, *No way! The odds of that happening are too great!* If—and this is a very big IF—only one, two, or three such random genetic changes were to be found in the natural world, our minds could accept it. However, it is obvious that for a simple cell—that somehow got a spark of life millions of years ago—to be changed into many millions of species with hundreds of millions of marvelous traits, something had to be happening besides a hundred million chances and accidents.

The stupendous amount of variety that our Father of details has placed on this earth can really only be explained in terms of design and purpose. The tremendous number of genetic changes required to turn a single cell into millions of species—all by random chance—is simply beyond mathematical possibility. But since some people are determined to not believe in God, they have to explain away the miraculous power of God, using wording that subtly turns the human mind away from Him. Be aware of this subtlety when you are reading books, magazines, and newspapers published by unbelievers.

---

1   http://news.nationalgeographic.com/news/2005/02/0218_050218_human_diet_2.html

Me? Eat Your Fruits?

Drosophila melanogaster, the **common fruit flies**, are the little bugs that appear out of nowhere to swarm around fruit left on a countertop. They are attracted to the alcohol created by the breakdown of sugars in the rotting fruit, and they can squeeze through an ordinary window screen. Once a female fruit fly locates some rotting fruit or sap, she lays several hundred eggs in it, which hatch in twelve to fifteen hours.

The larvae grow for about four days, feeding on the sweet food source. Then they go through metamorphosis in four more days and emerge as adults. Females can mate within twelve hours of emerging, allowing an entire new generation of fruit flies to be produced in less than ten days, although cooler temperatures slow down the process. No wonder some people in ancient times thought the common fruit fly was spontaneously produced from rotting produce!

Because of their rapid reproduction rates, various species from the *Drosophila* genus are often used in genetic studies—*D. melanogaster* is the most popular species for this. Some 7,000 people worldwide currently earn their full-time income studying these little flies. If that has been going on for fifteen years, it means over 100,000 years have been spent studying the common fruit fly, and many of its mysteries are still unsolved!

Drosophila is Latin for "dew-loving," with dew referring to the sweet sap or rotting fruit juice the fruit fly loves. The larvae feed on molds growing on the fermenting juices. *Melanogaster* is a Latin compound meaning "black belly."

The compound eye of *Drosophila melanogaster* contains 760 **ommatidia**, or individual units. No, I didn't count them, I am using a figure from someone else's study! Another study concluded that the common fruit fly uses two-thirds of its tiny brain just to process images.

With wings that beat 220 times a second, the fruit fly can reportedly do a ninety-degree turn in fifty milliseconds. By my calculations, that means it could rotate in five complete circles in about the same time you can say Mississippi!

SPECIES #48

KINGDOM: Animalia
PHYLUM: Arthropoda
CLASS: Insecta
ORDER: Diptera
FAMILY: Drosophilidae
GENUS: *Drosophila*
SPECIES: *melanogaster*

Of Chitin and Iridescence

Chitin is the substance that makes up the hard parts of bugs. The word comes from the Greek *citwn,* or covering, perhaps in reference to its role in the covering, or exoskeleton, of insects.

Chitin is also responsible for the brilliant colors of many insects. Though it has no pigment of its own, chitin reflects light in unusual ways due to the extremely thin layers it forms (often only a few microns, or thousandths of an inch, thick). Some layers of chitin are actually thinner than the wavelength of light. Depending on how thick the tiny layers and threads of chitin are, light shining on the insect reflects back in brilliant colors. This effect is known as iridescence, or structural color. Insects are not unique in producing iridescence: peacocks, blue jays, cat eyes at night, soap bubbles, CDs, and oil on water also produce iridescent coloring. The intense iridescent blue of the blue morpho butterfly is visible against jungle treetops by pilots flying half a mile above it.

Iridescence combined with natural pigmentation can result in intricate, shifting displays of color. For example, consider an insect with a layer of brown beneath the iridescent chitin layer. The insect appears brown until direct light hits the chitin, when it suddenly changes to florescent green. As it moves and the angle of the light source changes, a blue sheen explodes on the surface. Moments later it turns purple. Remove the light source, and it returns to its normal brown.

SPECIES #49

KINGDOM: Animalia
PHYLUM: Arthropoda
CLASS: Insecta
ORDER: Coleoptera
FAMILY: Scarabaeidae
GENUS: Melolonthinae
SPECIES: *phyllophaga*

Hold Still, Mom!

"April showers bring May flowers; May flowers bring June bugs." So goes the ditty of my childhood days. I learned that there are several hundred species in the genus *Melolonthinae*.

My wife helped with this project by bringing in specimens from time to time, and when this June bug landed on her head one evening, she patiently held still while we ran for the camera. This was before we acquired better lenses, and the poor **June bug** later became the subject of many test photos with various lens configurations until I finally realized that to do consistent macro photography for publication, I simply needed a dedicated macro lens. Unfortunately, by the time I acquired the lens, this specimen had seen better days. In spite of the number of photos we shot of him, we somehow ended up without any good macro shots.

One feature of June bugs that struck me is that the ventral (belly) side is often hairy. I had always thought of June bugs as hard creatures, but when I took the time to look closely, they are teddy bear furry on the underside. Our Father of details has many surprises for us if we look closely!

Sky Hanger

The image on the previous page of an unidentified **long-jawed orb weaver** species is one of the few photos we took in the wild that turned out well. This species was stretched out upside down from its nearly invisible web near a potato flower, waiting for an unsuspecting pollinator to check out the blossom. Squint a bit and imagine you are a nectar-craving pollinator flitting from flower to flower. Caught up in the thrill of a sweet harvest, you could easily miss the silent predator waiting at the next stop.

Obviously, this family of spiders earned its common name as a result of its extra-long *chelicerae*, commonly called jaws by non-specialists. These jaws are sometimes longer than the spider's head.

Unlike some other spiders, long-jawed orb weavers do not attach a signal thread to their bodies to alert them by tugging when something hits the web. They rely on sight to detect entangled prey. Since the web is not sticky, the long-jawed orb weaver must jump and grab its victim quickly before it recovers from the surprise of slamming into the unseen strands of silk.

Long-jawed orb weavers often live near water. In fact, they can walk on water faster than on land! Long-jawed orb weavers, unlike other orb weavers, often leave the centers of their webs open, and they build with fewer *radii* (spokes). All these variations were built in by our Father of details when He designed this species.

SPECIES #50

KINGDOM: Animalia
PHYLUM: Arthropoda
CLASS: Arachnida
ORDER: Araneae
FAMILY: Tetragnathidae
GENUS: Melolonthinae
SPECIES: *phyllophaga*

> SPECIES #51
> **KINGDOM:** Animalia
> **PHYLUM:** Arthropoda
> **CLASS:** Insecta (Insects)
> **ORDER:** Coleoptera
> **FAMILY:** Brentidae?
> **GENUS:** *Cylas?*
> **SPECIES:**

Which Weevil?

Is this a **sweet potato weevil**? I hope not! While the red thorax of this insect matches the description, it seems to lack the sweet potato weevil's reddish legs. Did this specimen happen to be in the wrong light to see its red legs? Is it really a sweet potato weevil? I was pleased to find a free digital weevil identification guide, but dismayed to discover that it has 677 pages (and that's just for the state of Kansas). Identifying this weevil would not be easy.

This seemed to be a snouted weevil of the Brentidae family, but there are 3,500 Brentidae species in the United States alone. However, I noticed that the Brentidae family has straight antennae, while this specimen has bent antennae. That means it belongs to the Curculionidae family, with 40,000 species worldwide.

The snout on weevils is designed for the same purpose as the snout on a hog—for digging. Weevils dig into sweet potatoes. They dig into soil. They dig into stored grain. They dig and eat and destroy. If I remember right, this specimen escaped without being captured or killed. Even if it isn't a sweet potato weevil, I don't like the thought of it reproducing in my garden.

Garden Guard

Miss Muffet could hardly be blamed for abandoning her curds and whey if a **banded garden spider** suddenly dropped on the tuffet beside her! Although *Argiope trifasciata* carries toxins like most spiders, it is harmless to humans. The genus name is Latin for "silver-faced," while the species name refers to the three colors on its back: yellow, black, and white.

The garden spider can spin its web in only one hour. Then it waits head-down to pounce on the first unfortunate insect that hits the web. A garden spider can eat prey twice its size, and a related species is even known to have eaten a small bat that became entangled in its web. To subdue its meal, the spider quickly wraps it in silk and injects it with toxins to kill it and soften the hard body parts.

One interesting characteristic of spiders in the *Argiope* genus is the **stabilimentum**, or web decoration, they usually place in the web. In this photo the stabilimentum appears at the bottom center of the web. The purpose of the stabilimentum is not well understood. Originally, scientists assumed they were used to stabilize the web, but researchers have since abandoned this theory. The stabilimentum reflects ultraviolet light, which may help ensnare some insects that are attracted to ultraviolet light. However, one study found that webs without any stabilimenta trapped 37 percent more insects than webs with them. However, birds also seemed less likely to fly through the webs with stabilimenta. So is the stabilimentum an insect attractant, a bird repellent, or something else? The answer is still up in the air!

The male spider builds a web near the female, waiting until she goes through her last instar and matures. Once she matures, he quickly mates with her—before her palps harden enough to eat him!

SPECIES #52

KINGDOM: Animalia
PHYLUM: Arthropoda
CLASS: Arachnida
ORDER: Araneae
FAMILY: Araneidae
GENUS: *Argiope*
SPECIES: *trifasciata*

Brightening Fall Days

This bright **orange marbled orb weaver** is often seen crawling along the ground in the fall, around Halloween, which gives it eerie associations for some people. Earlier in the year, it is more of a dull grayish color. Of course, our Father of details created this colorful spider long before the appearance of Halloween's pagan traditions. True to its nature, we found this excellent specimen crawling in the grass in late October. This is a female, probably searching for a good spot to lay her eggs.

Like most of the other 10,000 orb weaver species, this one rebuilds the sticky part of its web every day! However, while some orb weavers wait on the web for prey, the marbled orb weaver often hides nearby, with a single strand of silk running from its body to the center of the web. As soon as something hits the web, the signal thread tugs on the spider, and it knows something has been caught. The spider then scurries to the web and subdues the prey.

If you see an orb weaver in your yard, consider it your friend. They are harmless to humans and dangerous to bugs, making them an asset to your garden.

SPECIES #53

KINGDOM: Animalia
PHYLUM: Arthropoda
CLASS: Arachnida
ORDER: Araneae
FAMILY: Araneidae
GENUS: Araneus
SPECIES: marmoreus

Master of Disguise

This **large maple spanwood moth** is hard to identify; I almost confused it with the confused eusarca. I do not guarantee my identification. The identification guides list two other similar-looking species in addition to the confused eusarca.

If you see a twig moving on the ground, look carefully. You may find that it is not a stick being moved by the wind, but a large maple spanworm caterpillar or a similar species moving on its little feet. The simplicity of this moth gives it an elegance of its own.

SPECIES #54

KINGDOM: Animalia
PHYLUM: Arthropoda
CLASS: Insecta
ORDER: Lepidoptera
FAMILY: Geometridae
GENUS: *Prochoerodes*
SPECIES: *lineola*

The large maple spanworm caterpillar is clearly the handiwork of a skilled Designer.

SPECIES #55

KINGDOM: Animalia
PHYLUM: Arthropoda
CLASS: Insecta
ORDER: Coleoptera
FAMILY: Chrysomelidae
GENUS: *Leptinotarsa*
SPECIES: *decemlineata*

Beetle Bombs

If you count the lines on a **Colorado potato beetle**, you will find the reason for the species name *decemlineata*. *Decem* means "ten," while *lineata* means "lined." Common names include ten-striped spearman, ten-lined potato beetle, or simply potato bug.

In spite of its attractive pinstriped paint job, this Colorado potato beetle is probably considered ugly by most gardeners, since it can quickly make a mess of a garden. Interestingly, it seems not to have eaten potato plants until European settlers, having adopted potatoes from South America centuries earlier, introduced potatoes into the beetle's home territory in northern Mexico and the southwest United States. Once the beetles were introduced to potatoes in about 1840, they soon spread all the way to Europe and Asia.

During the early days of the Cold War, propaganda in several European countries blamed the potato beetle outbreak on a plot by the CIA to destroy the food supply of Communist Europe. The East German government spread a story about a farmer who noticed two American planes flying overhead and found his fields swarming with potato beetles a few days later. There is no evidence that the beetles were introduced intentionally. Most likely they arrived with potatoes shipped to U.S. armies during the World Wars.

In an effort to halt the "invasion," citizens, including schoolchildren after school, were asked to volunteer to pick the beetles, drowning them in buckets of chemicals. However, the beetle population survived and continues eating potatoes in Europe and Asia to this day.

All eradication efforts against the Colorado potato beetle have failed. DDT was used heavily in the early 1900s and was partially successful until the beetles became resistant to it. Since then, the Colorado potato beetle has adapted to resist all major pesticides. The best organic attack plan for a gardener is to do what the East German schoolchildren did—walk through the garden and handpick each beetle. Inspecting for and picking off the beetles regularly, beginning early in the season, can reduce their numbers enough to allow a good harvest.

One Colorado potato beetle can eat six square inches of potato leaf every day. Females lay up to eight hundred eggs, which mature in a few weeks, giving the beetles the potential to wreak massive destruction quickly. A few females and a long growing season can turn a beautiful row of potatoes into ugly bare stalks. No wonder these fancy, pinstriped beetles are not welcome in gardens!

Immature potato bugs look entirely different from the mature form. A war on these little fellows gives a head start in the war on the species.

This Cold War era poster claimed "Imperialists" were dropping potato bugs on fields. The fight against these pests was presented as a fight for peace.

SPECIES #56

KINGDOM: Animalia
PHYLUM: Arthropoda
CLASS: Arachnida
ORDER: Araneae
FAMILY: Tetragnathidae
GENUS: *Leucauge*
SPECIES: *venusta*

Another Elegant Spider

The **orchard spider** is another long-jawed orb weaver. The Latin species name *venusta* means "attractive, elegant, or charming." The bright green legs next to the white, yellow, and black body markings do give this species a charming splash of color. I noticed that the mix of colors also camouflaged it well. Orb weavers are said to have three claws on each foot, and it would be interesting to take a close look at one. Unfortunately, I was not able to preserve this specimen.

This photo is an example of the huge amount of patience required to photograph wild specimens. Besides the web's tendency to move in the slightest breeze, making focus difficult or impossible, I was leaning over a porch railing, so I had to take a handheld shot without a tripod. I suppose the best thing I can offer is an apology for a less-than-perfect photo. I'm sorry! As unsuccessful deer hunters are apt to say, maybe next year.

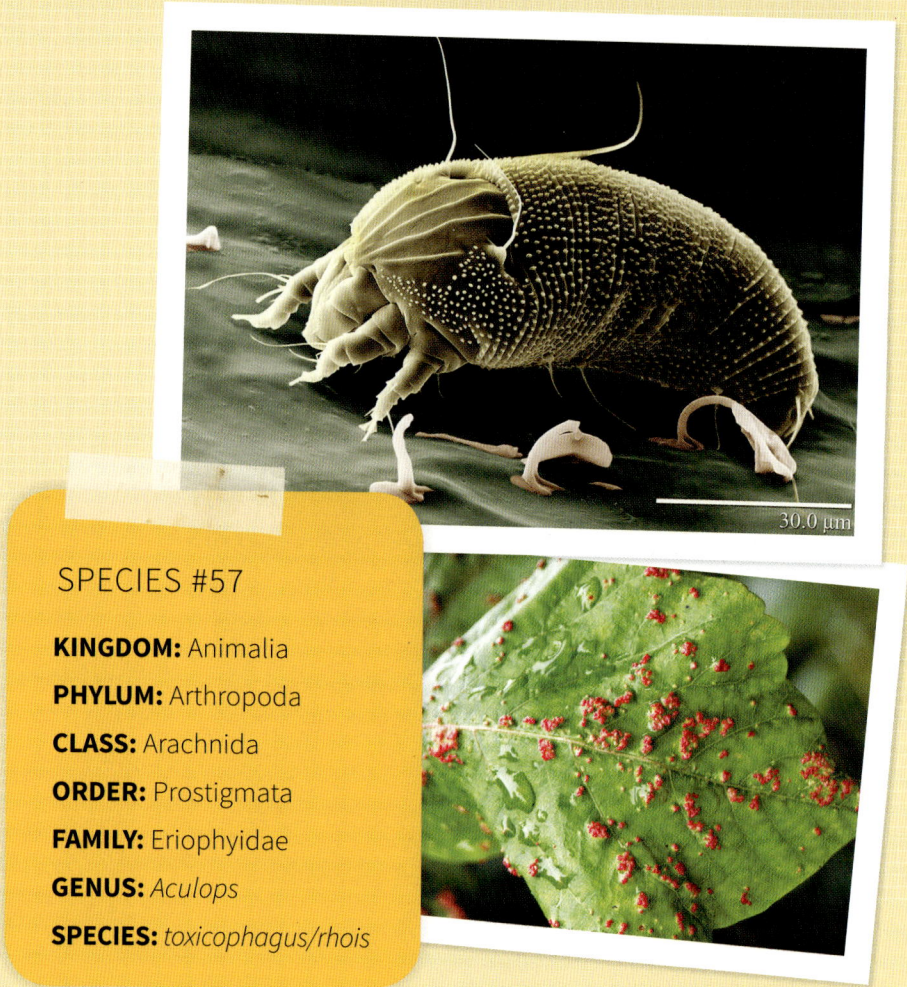

SPECIES #57

KINGDOM: Animalia
PHYLUM: Arthropoda
CLASS: Arachnida
ORDER: Prostigmata
FAMILY: Eriophyidae
GENUS: *Aculops*
SPECIES: *toxicophagus/rhois*

Itty-Bitty Mites

You may be wondering why this photo of a poison ivy plant is accompanied with a label from the animal kingdom. Good observation! The species referenced is the animal that caused the small red galls on the leaf, the **poison ivy leaf gall mite**. I couldn't find a photo of this species, so I have included an electron microscope photo of the related rust mite, *Aceria anthocoptes*. Notice the scale on the photo—the total length of this specimen is about one-tenth of a millimeter! Its tiny size allows the poison ivy leaf gall mite to spread from plant to plant on wind currents.

The poison ivy mite is in the class Arachnida, the same class as the spiders. In the Eriophyidae family, the gall mites, we find 3,600 known species, with one source estimating that this may account for only 10 percent of the actual number! The species name translates as "poison eater," an apt name for a mite that lives on a poison ivy plant.

Eighty-Seven Pulses Per Second

When I saw this cricket's species name, *exclamationis*, I wondered if that meant it sings with an exclamation point at the end. My surmise was wrong; the name comes from the inverted "exclamation mark," at the base of its antennae (see inset). The common name, **Davis's tree cricket**, is from the first describer of the species, William Thompson Davis.

When this cricket sings, it produces 87 pulses per second at a pitch of 2.7 kilohertz. A similar species, the narrow-winged tree cricket, sings at 112 pulses per second and has antennae markings that look more like a J. Details, details, details!

SPECIES #58

KINGDOM: Animalia
PHYLUM: Arthropoda
CLASS: Insecta
ORDER: Orthoptera
FAMILY: Gryllidae
GENUS: Oecanthus
SPECIES: exclamationis

SPECIES #59

KINGDOM: Animalia
PHYLUM: Arthropoda
CLASS: Arachnida
ORDER: Araneae
FAMILY: Pisauridae
GENUS: *Dolomedes*
SPECIES:

Hydrophobics That Fear No Water

The **fishing spider** lives mostly on land, but it can also dive into the water and stay submerged for a while, only to pop out again completely dry. This amazing feat is enabled by the hydrophobic hairs that cover its body. The fishing spider can even walk on the surface of the water without wetting its feet!

Hydrophobia translates literally as "the fear of water"; however, hydrophobia is also used as a technical term for chemical repulsion, or lack of attraction, to water. When the fishing spider dives into water, its fine hydrophobic hairs trap a layer of air all around its body, allowing it to pop out of the water with its skin dry.

The fishing spider breathes with **book lungs**, gill-like structures on its body that do the same job as our lungs. When the fishing spider is submerged, its book lungs breathe the trapped air layer around its body. So although the fishing spider is covered with hydrophobic hair, it has no fear of water—in fact, it loves water. Who but our Father of details could have made a spider with a built-in oxygen tank and wet suit, capable of walking on water!

Somehow this specimen ended up in our collection of dried spiders. There is a reason you only see a face shot here. As I mentioned, spiders don't dry well, and this one's body is pretty shriveled. I did not know this was a fishing spider until I took a photo of its eye configuration. We do not have any standing water sources on our two acres other than a few watering troughs, so how this fishing spider ended up here is a mystery that only our Father of details can answer. Perhaps He just wanted a fishing spider to end up in this journal.

This cricket spiracle valve is enlarged about 350 times by a scanning electron microscope. Electron microscopes show fine detail but no color.

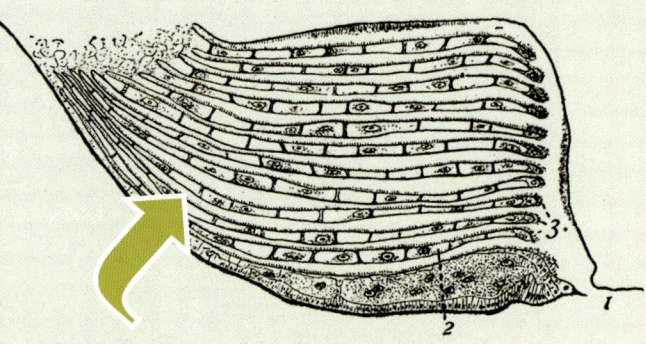

This book lung drawing by John Henry Comstock shows: (1) the lung slit, (2) the space filled with blood, (3) the leaves of the book lung.

Lung Lessons

Breathing Without Lungs

Insects and some spiders are **apulmonates**, meaning they have no lungs. Unlike animals with lungs, which take in oxygen and mix it with blood to distribute it throughout their bodies, apulmonates take in oxygen and vent carbon dioxide using a **tracheal system**, a branching network of increasingly fine air tubes that deliver oxygen directly to each cell. These tubes have a wire-like substance in the walls that works like the wire in a clothes dryer hose to keep them from kinking and collapsing. In some species, sections of the trachea can be squeezed shut to make balloon-like areas that hold oxygen. This allows the animal to store air, either to use under water or to slow down dehydration. Aquatic insects also use these air pockets to provide buoyancy. Imagine being able to suck in air and use that trapped air as a life jacket to keep you afloat!

The tracheal system gets its oxygen through **spiracle valves**, openings in the insect's skin on each body segment that can close and open as needed.

Lungs like a Book

Spiders with lungs, called **pulmonates**, breath with book lungs. The lungs are layered like the pages of a book, somewhat like gills on fish. However, instead of taking oxygen from water like fish gills, book lungs take oxygen from the air, like our lungs. However, scientists say the oxygen transfer in book lungs functions differently from our lungs.

One-Way Lungs

Studying the lungs of these little creatures made me aware of what I will call "the bird lung problem." Bird lungs must function under demanding conditions, supplying hard-working flight muscles with the oxygen they need even at high altitudes where the air is thinner. To meet this need, our Father of details gave birds an ingenious one-way lung. But how can a lung be one-way? Easy! Just loop the air circuit and add some bellows that take in air and hold it until the air needs to move, and the bird can be taking in oxygen even while it is exhaling!

By this means, air is continually moving through a bird's lungs, enabling it to fly at high altitudes where oxygen is sparse. The diagrams below illustrate the avian respiratory system better than I can explain it in writing.

Have you ever pondered how you would have solved the problem of providing oxygen to cells and carrying away the carbon dioxide in various species, on land, in air, and in the sea? Lungs, tracheal tubes, book lungs, one-way lungs . . . our Father of details has created diverse means to nourish living cells with oxygen and discharge the carbon dioxide. His designs are marvelous!

The illustrations below show how a bird gets fresh oxygen even while exhaling. The red lines indicate fresh air, and the blue lines indicate used air. The green arrows show the expansion and contraction of the air sacs. If birds had lungs like humans, they could not get enough oxygen at high altitudes.

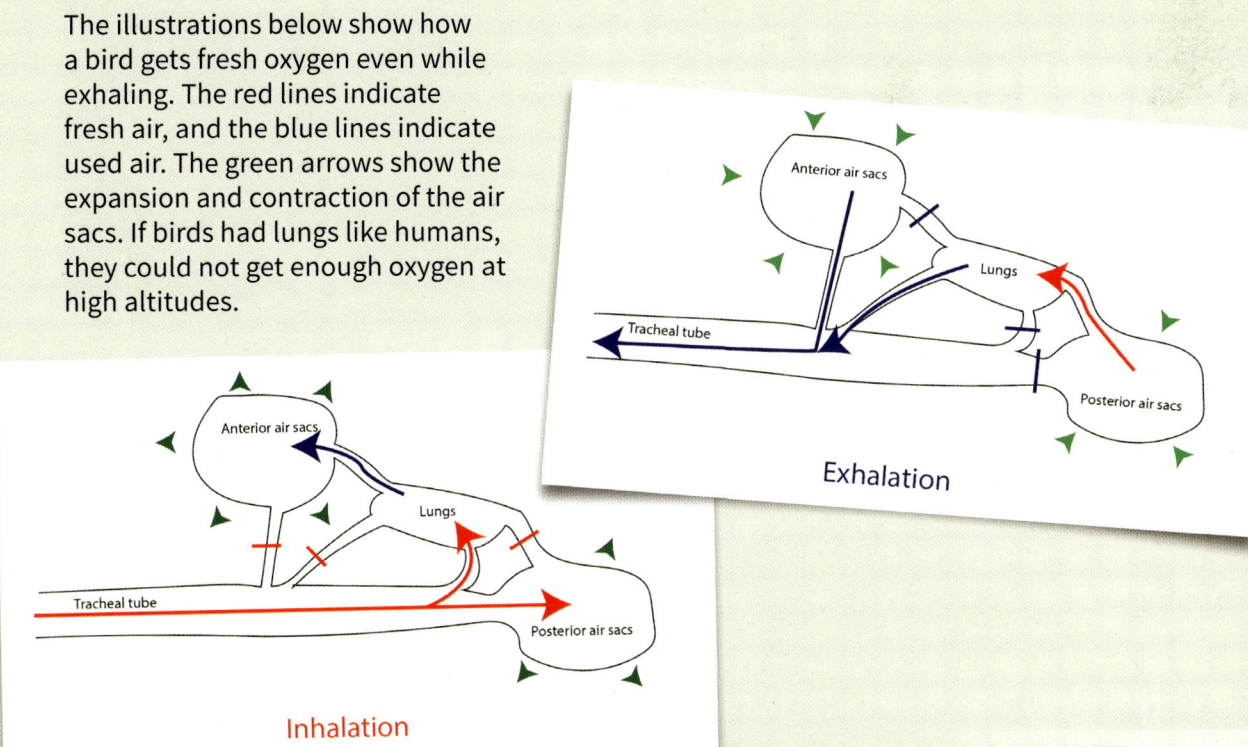

Another Test

Quick! Name six differences between katydids, grasshoppers, and crickets.

1. A grasshopper has short antennae, while katydids and crickets have antennae that are usually longer than their bodies.
2. Katydids have tympana, or ears, on the tibia of their forelegs; and the *tarsi*, the end part of the leg, has four segments. If the tibia has no tympanum, but the tarsi has four segments, the insect is one of the camel or Jerusalem crickets, or a leafroller. If it has a three-segmented tarsi with long antennae, it is a cricket.
3. Cricket songs tend to be more regular and less raspy than katydid songs, making crickets sound more musical.
4. Grasshoppers sing by rubbing the hind leg against the wing; katydids and crickets sing by rubbing their forewings together.
5. Grasshoppers are herbivorous (plant-eating), while some katydids and crickets are omnivorous (eating both plants and animals).
6. Female grasshoppers have short ovipositors, while katydids and crickets have long ones.

If you knew those six points without doing some research, you knew more than I did!

With more than 6,400 species of katydids, I am at a loss to identify the specimen on the previous page. The long ovipositor indicates that this is a female. She will use this ovipositor to lay her eggs, pushing it into a crack in a plant.

If you look closely, you can count the four segments of the tarsi. Note that the head lost most of its vibrant green color as it dried. The photo on pages 138–139 may be the same species as the green one in the small photo on the bottom of the next page, but I think I can see some difference in head shape. What do you think?

Is the dark brown specimen on the next page a katydid or a cricket? It is not a grasshopper, since it has long antennae. I would guess it is a cricket due to its color, but that's just a guess. To be certain, we would need to count the tarsi and check the foretibia for a tympanum.

Is the green specimen on the next page a cricket or a katydid? We see a four-segmented tarsi, so it's most likely a katydid.

Now, what is the light brown insect? The long antenna (one is broken) tells us this is a katydid or cricket, but it's hard to tell which, since this may be an immature specimen. I happened to see this insect while I contemplated photographing the dried flower head. Lo and behold, this insect was hiding inside, along with several more. Our Father of details gave this species an excellent camouflage and a snug, safe refuge from predators.

SPECIES #60

KINGDOM: Animalia
PHYLUM: Arthropoda
CLASS: Insecta
ORDER: Orthoptera
FAMILY: Tettigoniidae
GENUS:
SPECIES:

Comma or Question Mark?

Without looking at the scientific name, can you tell me if this is a comma butterfly or a question mark butterfly? See that comma-shaped mark on the underside of the wing? You guessed it; it's a comma. If a dot were present below that mark, it would be a different species, the question mark butterfly. So many little details! Our Father of details seems to delight in His creativity, adding a splash here, a mark there, or a different number of segments in an antenna.

The differences between insect species can seem meaningless until you consider the visible differences between larger animal species. For example, a black bear and a brown bear do not appear very different at first glance. The brown bear is brown instead of black, generally larger, and has a slightly different skull shape. Shrink those same three attributes to the size of

SPECIES #61

KINGDOM: Animalia
PHYLUM: Arthropoda
CLASS: Insecta
ORDER: Lepidoptera
FAMILY: Nymphalidae
GENUS: Polygonia
SPECIES:

a butterfly, and they may be harder to see, but they are enough to make two insect species distinct from each other.

The **eastern comma butterfly** is a beautiful piece of art. I was sorely disappointed when I pulled out the drying pins to photograph this specimen. Though I had covered the wings with a waxy paper to avoid losing the scales, I found that somehow many scales had still been lost in the pinning process. He was so beautiful when I pinned him! Were this a science book, this specimen would be too damaged to include, but this is the journal of a backyard safari, so our blunders must be included as well as our successes.

Note that the underside of this butterfly is well camouflaged. Sunning itself on a leaf like the one in our garden, the eastern comma can seemingly disappear just by closing its wings.

These creatures are tough to catch! While butterflies in general are wary, this species seems especially so. Another larger specimen eluded my net many times, leaving me with a wad of grape or squash leaves in the net instead.

Rather than sucking nectar from flowers, eastern comma butterflies feed on sap, rotting fruit, and minerals gained from puddling. There are usually two generations per year. The earlier generation is darker in color than the later one. The second generation, emerging later in summer, overwinters in sheltered places, though some may migrate south.

Eastern comma butterfly larvae tend to feed on false nettles and elm leaves. The left photo on page 142 is a close-up shot of the comma, with the antenna tip inset. What neat "shingles"!

Out to Grab a Lunch!

What do you call a funnel web spider that lives in the grass? A **grass spider**. (My photos were taken on a shrub, not on grass, however.) While they look and act a lot like barn funnel weavers, grass spiders have a different eye pattern and prefer making their webs in grass or bushes.[1]

The evergreens right outside our front door are home to quite a few of these agile spiders. If you approach and peek into the funnel, the spider vanishes into the interior of the shrub. But if prey lands on its non-sticky web, it rushes out and pounces on it before its victim untangles itself. To entice one out of the funnel hole, stand off to the side where you are not noticeable and tickle the web with a piece of grass. Often the spider will feel the vibrations and rush out looking for lunch. Turn to page 40 to see how this same technique is used by a jumping spider to lure his lunch *out* of the funnel.

---

[1] I am not sure of the species name for this specimen because there are several others that are similar, but since this is a common species, I figured it was close enough.

SPECIES #62

KINGDOM: Animalia
PHYLUM: Arthropoda
CLASS: Arachnida
ORDER: Araneae
FAMILY: Agelenidae
GENUS: *Agelenopsis*
SPECIES: *pennsylvanica*

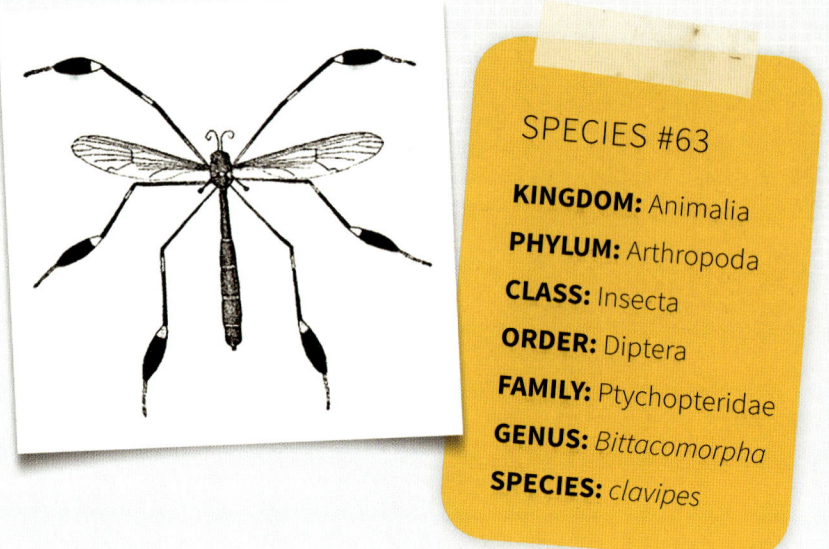

SPECIES #63

KINGDOM: Animalia
PHYLUM: Arthropoda
CLASS: Insecta
ORDER: Diptera
FAMILY: Ptychopteridae
GENUS: *Bittacomorpha*
SPECIES: *clavipes*

Vanishing Fly

Phantom crane flies—which are not true crane flies—earned their name from their mysterious way of floating through the air, usually near the ground. A crane fly not only flies with its short wings, but also extends its legs to catch an extra boost from the breeze. When a phantom crane fly passes over a light area, it may look like just a series of black, disconnected patches. Then it glides into a dark region and seems to dissolve into a cloud of white spots drifting along. In the right conditions, it may appear to blend into a greyish smudge.

Like true crane flies, adult phantom crane flies do not seem to eat much. Once the eggs are fertilized, the female lays them near a wet spot, often in shallow water with rotting debris on the bottom. The eggs hatch and the larvae float near the surface of the water, using a long tracheal tube like a snorkel for breathing.

When Daniel came in all excited with this new find, we had to add it to our journal. Its bulging **basitarsi** (the leg right above the "ankle" joint) and the alternating bands of black and white on the legs give this species a unique beauty. Like its crane fly cousins, this species' legs are hard to keep connected to the body. I tried really, really hard to keep all the legs intact on this specimen. I managed to get a small mounting pin through its very small body and spread the legs to dry. After a week or so, I gently pulled the pin out of the Styrofoam to prepare for photographs, but somehow all the legs on one side were bumped off in the process. Of the three legs left, only one still has the full "foot." I decided to leave the mounting pin in, lest I end up with a totally legless specimen.

Leaving Leopard

The **giant leopard moth**[1] is named for its striking color scheme of black spots on a white background and for its relatively large wingspan, up to three inches. However, we found this caterpillar to be leopard-like in another way—its quickness to disappear. When handled, it rolls into an unresponsive ball, bristles pointing out on all sides. Tap the bristles lightly to spin it thirty to sixty degrees, or tap it repeatedly to make it spin in a circle. Then turn your back for a few minutes and see if this dormant-looking caterpillar stays put. This one disappeared from the worktable twice when I briefly left it unattended. One time it was gone for a week before turning up in the dining room among some sacks. The other time I didn't leave it as long, and we found it nearby.

Unlike some hairy caterpillars whose spines can sting, the giant leopard moth larva is harmless. Adults can emit a foul-smelling yellow substance from their eyes when handled, as a deterrent to predators.

The adult appears snowy white, speckled with black leopard-like rings and spots that look like bright blue eyes. I don't remember ever seeing a moth like this before. The bluish colors are produced by iridescence. In most views from the top, only the two larger spots on the side of the head give off the blue glow, appearing like blue eyes. Underneath the snowy wings is an abdomen with red stripes and blue-green iridescent shapes. Our Father of details can do wonders with a little light and a little moth!

---

[1] Though the caterpillar pictured here is from our property, the moth is not.

SPECIES #64

KINGDOM: Animalia
PHYLUM: Arthropoda
CLASS: Insecta
ORDER: Lepidoptera
FAMILY: Erebidae
GENUS: Hypercompe
SPECIES: scribonia

The giant leopard moth pupa.

The iridescent adult moth.

Another Test!

Do you know the main differences between butterflies and moths?
1. Butterflies are diurnal, flying during the day, while moths are nocturnal, flying at night.
2. Butterflies have clubbed antennae, meaning they end in a ball or club shape. Moths have various types of antennae, either smooth or feathery, with very few having a club.
3. Butterflies form a hard chrysalis (from the Greek root *khrysos*, meaning "gold," the color of many chrysalises), while moth caterpillars usually spin a silk cocoon.
4. Butterfly bodies are thin and smooth, while moth bodies are thick and fuzzy.
5. When resting, butterflies hold their wings vertically, while moths hold their wings flat.
6. Butterflies tend to be brightly colored, while moths tend to be drab. However, this last difference is a very general rule, with many exceptions.

None of these rules are consistent in every case, but the exceptions to the first five are few. The easiest rule is number one: If it flies by day, it's a butterfly; if it flies at night, it's a moth. If you find one flying at daybreak and sunset, you may need to fall back on rule number two or four!

Slippery Carpet Layer

What walks on one foot and lays out its own carpet as it goes? Of course you figured it out from the pictures on these pages. **Slugs** are essentially snails without shells, or with only partial shells. With an estimated 60,000 to 80,000 species of gastropods (slugs and snails) crawling this planet, this is no small class of animals! The class name Gastropoda translates as "stomach-footed," based on a past mistaken belief that the entrails of the slug were in the part that drags along the ground. Actually, the intestines are located mostly under the mantle, and the bottom of the slug is really a foot, or something akin to it.

If I remember right, we found this specimen in the compost pile. Most slugs feed on decomposing matter, although some go after living greens, making them garden pests. Some even eat flesh. Like earthworms, slugs are **hermaphrodites**, meaning they have both male and female reproductive organs. While they can reproduce by themselves, they prefer having a mate.

Oozing out a layer of slime may not seem much like laying out a carpet, but the purpose is the same. Carpet pads our feet, while the slime laid out by a slug protects its foot as it slides along. Not only does the slime protect the slug from rough surfaces, it also contains fibers that help keep the

The pneumostome, slightly visible above the point of this arrow, is a breathing hole sort of like a whale's.

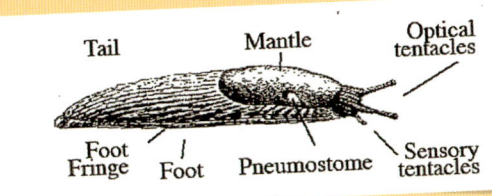

slug from slipping down slopes (see photo to the right). Imagine, a substance that reduces friction and provides traction at the same time! In addition to helping with mobility, the slime trail provides a way for slugs of the same species to find one another. Carnivorous slugs also follow the trail so they can eat the slug laying it.

The species box reveals that we do not know exactly which species we found. In fact, even the genus is in question. I sent photos to a slug specialist at the University of Kentucky for identification help, but he only offered suggestions. Slugs vary greatly in color, which may be affected by their diet. It's possible that this is an albino specimen (note the unusual white tentacles), or even a newly discovered species. In the world of small creatures, there remains much to discover. If some day you are browsing a slug identification manual and come across something called *Arion atnipensis*, you'll know we did indeed find a new species!

Before moving on, note the tentacles—the upper pair has what looks like eyeballs. Yes, they are used for vision, but slugs actually depend more on the lower "feeling" pair for getting information about their environment.

SPECIES #65
KINGDOM: Animalia
PHYLUM: Mollusca
CLASS: Gastropoda
ORDER: Sigmurethra
FAMILY: Arionidae
GENUS: *Arion*
SPECIES:

Silk Recycler

Furrow orb weavers (sometimes just called furrow spiders) are great recyclers! They eat their web and recycle the silk, sometimes daily. When an unfortunate victim lands on the new web, the spider immobilizes it with a venomous bite, wraps it in silk, and carries it off the web. (While these spiders can bite humans, they are not considered dangerous.) Like many other spider species, the furrow orb weaver injects enzymes into the victim to soften up hard parts so they can be easily digested later. Very little waste is left from a spider's dinner.

Although it's gray rather than orange, this species appears to be closely related to the marbled orb weaver. However, these lookalikes are often not as closely related as they appear. While both spiders are in the family Araneidae, they belong to different genera.

Researchers are finding that many taxonomic assignments laid down a century or two ago make no sense when details of the species are studied more closely; hence, researchers are constantly revising the taxonomy. It is no easy job to revise taxonomy; sometimes an agreement among the experts takes many years. Our Father of details isn't really concerned about man's naming conventions. I surmise that He just created them with little concern about how they fit into taxonomic categories. In fact, some species He created seem to defy neat categorization!

This specimen made its home on the outside of our kitchen window. My wife isn't particularly fond of spiders, but we instructed her to let this one be for a while so we could observe it. It exhibited typical furrow orb weaver behavior. During the day it was usually nowhere to be seen, hiding in the cracks of the window slides. Then at night it would appear to wrap and eat the victims. This specimen seemed to dine well on moths attracted to the lights in the house.

Although this species doesn't seem to like direct sunlight, I did find one eating breakfast one morning in broad daylight. I suppose it was willing to tolerate the sun to enjoy a meal.

This species is another example of the use of pheromones for attracting mates. When the female is ready, she builds a cocoon and emits pheromones. The male senses the pheromones through chemoreceptors and finds his way to her "nest." The female lays her eggs in the cocoon, and both parents may guard the nest—if the female doesn't eat the male!

Reference books indicate that the *cornutus* species prefers wet areas and is abundant along the shores of Lake Erie, one hundred miles north of our two acres. Although this summer was exceptionally rainy, the outside of our kitchen window is not a wet area, so apparently they can live in drier areas as well. This species appears to overwinter better than many other spiders and is one of the first to appear in spring.

With their lifestyle of feeding on insects that are often considered pests by humans, these furrow orb weavers are beneficial.

SPECIES #66

KINGDOM: Animalia
PHYLUM: Arthropoda
CLASS: Arachnida
ORDER: Araneae
FAMILY: Araneidae
GENUS: *Larinioides*
SPECIES: *cornutus*

SPECIES #67

KINGDOM: Animalia
PHYLUM: Arthropoda
CLASS: Insecta
ORDER: Diptera
FAMILY: Stratiomyidae
GENUS: *Odontomyia*
SPECIES: *virgo*

Green Soldiers

It's an amazing world out there in the backyard! I never knew fluorescent green flies inhabited our acreage! Did I overlook these bright-bellied flies before, or is this simply the first one our Father of details sent my way? I suspect the former.

Soldier fly is the name of this family, a large one that includes some 2,700 species. *Virgo* is my educated guess for the species name.

I find the green halteres intriguing. You can see them in both photos. It would be interesting to see them whirling around in flight, but I suppose they move too rapidly to be anything but a light green blur.

Note the *holoptic* eyes of this specimen, which indicate it's probably a male. *Holoptic* means "complete vision," meaning that the eyes almost meet in the middle, forming one field of view. Females have *dichoptic* eyes. *Dichoptic* (two-part vision) means the eyes are far enough apart to have two separate fields of view. Whether one field of view or two, in my eyes this green flying machine is a real beauty, a masterpiece of the creative power of our Father of details!

Super Smellers

I was working on the collection one day when Daniel rushed in, saying, "Dad, look what I found!" This beetle's fan-shaped antennae were unusual enough that he knew we didn't have one in our large collection.

How this insect obtained the common name of **cedar beetle** is a mystery to me. Their preferred home is an elm tree, although they lay eggs in other species of trees as well. For all their uniqueness, it seems they have been studied very little.

The beetles in the family Rhipiceridae are parasites. The grubs feed on cicada nymphs underground, leaving behind only the empty shell of the cicada. After the beetle grubs mature into adults, they live only a couple of days.

SPECIES #68

KINGDOM: Animalia
PHYLUM: Arthropoda
CLASS: Insecta
ORDER: Coleoptera
FAMILY: Rhipiceridae
GENUS: *Sandalus*
SPECIES: *niger*

The males are thought to find the females by sensing their pheromones with those fancy fan-shaped antennae. After the male finds the female, she quickly lays her eggs in the bark of a tree, preferably in slits where a cicada has also laid eggs. The cedar beetles do not eat the cicada eggs, but by laying her eggs alongside them, the female beetle ensures her brood will have a nearby food source.

Once the eggs hatch, both the cicadas and the beetles head down the tree and into the ground. One study found that a female cedar beetle would lay eggs in a synthetic crevice, but only if a cicada had been there first. This suggests that the beetle can sense where cicadas have been and uses that ability to locate promising sites to lay her own eggs.

Note the tympanum, or "ear," on the tree cricket's leg.

SPECIES #69

KINGDOM: Animalia
PHYLUM: Arthropoda
CLASS: Insecta
ORDER: Orthoptera
FAMILY: Gryllidae
GENUS: Neoxabea
SPECIES: bipunctata

Amplifier Maker

I never knew there were white crickets in this world, let alone that more than one species of white cricket inhabited our two acres (see page 133). This is just one more example of the diversity our Father of details has created. Looking at the photo, it is easy to see how they got their common name of **two-spotted tree cricket**; however, only the females have the two large dark spots on their backs. (This specimen was originally lighter-colored but darkened as it dried. It is also missing its long antennae and half of its legs.)

These crickets seem to "know" a bit about acoustics. A male chews a hole in a leaf and then places its wings against the edges of the hole. Then, when it uses its wings to sing, the leaf serves as a soundboard to add volume. The long trill made by these crickets reminds me of a high-pitched buzzer.

Would it be possible for a cricket to discover that if it stuck its head through a hole in a leaf and sang, the noise would be amplified? Yes, the cricket could discover that, but it has no way to pass on this knowledge to its offspring, which it will probably never see. Of course, crickets don't understand acoustics. They were programmed by our Father of details to do what they do.

Little Killers

I had heard that there were various species of **mosquitoes**, so when it came time to photograph and identify a couple of specimens we had collected, I began exploring how to identify the species. I learned that Ohio has about sixty species of mosquitoes! I did find an identification key, but when I saw that identification depends on microscopic details like whether there is a clump of hair at the base of the *proboscis*, I simply gave up. Worldwide, there are fifteen hundred mosquito species and counting. They live everywhere on earth except the polar regions and a few isolated islands.

We are blessed to live in one of the highest areas in our community, and I don't remember getting even one mosquito bite last summer. Not far from here, near a swampy area, folks have to go inside at dusk, and they get swarmed in broad daylight.

Mosquitoes have killed more people than any other animal in the world has killed—about two million people per year. Technically, it isn't the mosquito that kills, but various diseases the female mosquito transfers in its saliva when it takes a blood meal. When a mosquito begins to push its sucking instruments into flesh, it inserts saliva along with them. The saliva itself is amazing. It contains substances to keep blood from clotting and plugging the proboscis, it prevents platelet gathering, and it reduces blood vessel constriction. All of these help the mosquito draw blood more effectively.

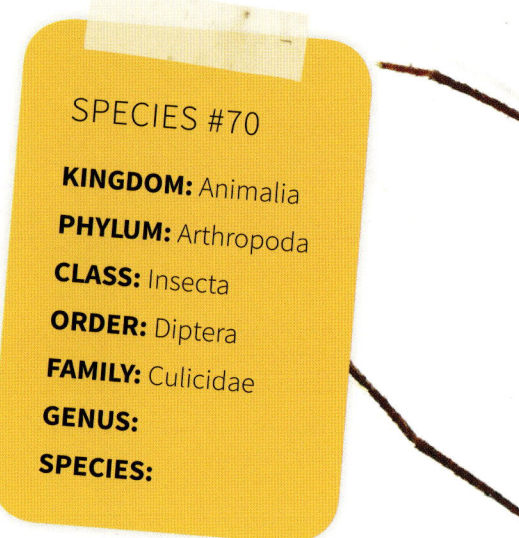

SPECIES #70

KINGDOM: Animalia
PHYLUM: Arthropoda
CLASS: Insecta
ORDER: Diptera
FAMILY: Culicidae
GENUS:
SPECIES:

This photo of a mosquito head reminds me of a Roman soldier! However, what looks like an eye is actually the base of a broken antenna. The real eye is the shrunken area ringed by orange dots.

In most species of mosquitoes, the female must drink some blood in order to grow eggs. Some species can lay the first batch of eggs without drinking blood, but require a blood meal to lay any more. Fewer than 10 percent of the mosquito species can develop eggs without a blood meal. Since male mosquitoes do not produce eggs, they do not feed on blood.

In addition to the blood they need for egg production, mosquitoes depend on sugar from nectar and plant juices. Mosquito saliva contains ingredients to help digest sugar, as well as antimicrobial agents so that the sugar doesn't start growing bacteria. The sugar is stored in the mosquito's crop and passed on to the stomach for digestion. The stomach is never allowed to be filled with sugar, because it needs to leave room in case a blood supply shows up. This ensures that there is always room for a drink of blood, since blood is harder to get than sugar. When the mosquito does get a drink of blood, it bypasses the crop and goes straight to the stomach.

Each detail of the mosquito was designed by our Father of details to make it an amazing creation. When man's sin brought death and disease into this world, the mosquito became a carrier of death. Will the next world have mosquitoes that do not carry diseases or cause bite wounds?

Busting a Mosquito Myth

While studying mosquitoes, I learned that a commonly repeated "fact" about them is actually a myth—purple martins, contrary to what most of us have heard, do not eat many mosquitoes. I know, many people and even some reputable books claim purple martins eat their weight in mosquitoes every day, or perhaps devour 2,000 mosquitoes daily. However, researchers who have actually examined the stomachs of purple martins have found that they rarely contain mosquitoes. In one study that did find mosquitoes in purple martin stomachs, the mosquitoes formed only about 3 percent of the diet.

If it isn't true, where did the story of purple martins' taste for mosquitoes originate? Biologists finally tracked the story down to J. L. Wade, a manufacturer of martin houses, who published a martin book in 1966[1] in which he took responsibility for originating the "2,000 mosquitoes per day" story and explained how he came up with the number. Since a purple martin's metabolic rate is very high, Wade estimated they would need to consume their weight in insects each day. He estimated that an average purple martin weighed four ounces, equal to 14,000 mosquitoes. Next he guessed that purple martins probably digested mosquitoes so rapidly that analyzing their stomach contents would be useless. Finally, to be on the conservative side, he gave an estimate of 2,000 mosquitoes per day—and the story took off.

Unfortunately, Wade's study was flawed in several ways. First, the average purple martin weighs one and three-quarter ounces, not four. Second, he had no evidence for his assumption that purple martins regularly consume mosquitoes. Third, he was wrong about his belief that analyzing their stomach contents would be useless, since some mosquito parts can make it through the entire digestive system intact. Fourth, his proposed number of mosquitos ingested was a guess without any evidence to back it up. And finally, he ignored the difference between the flying times of purple martins and mosquitoes, which only overlap a half hour morning and evening.

In areas where mosquito populations are naturally low, natural predators like purple martins, swallows, and especially bats may help control or even reduce the numbers, but for large infestations, chemical sprays are about the only effective control. DEET is a proven effective personal agent, while citronella oil seems to afford a weaker but more natural protection. Garlic and vitamin B12 pills have not been proven effective in clinical studies.

---

1 *What You Should Know About the Purple Martin: America's Most Wanted Bird*, Trio Manufacturing Co., Griggsville, Illinois, 1966.

The distinct wing patterns suggest that these two specimens are two different species of mosquitoes.

This thin-legged wolf spider is enjoying its meal of a housefly. Daniel enjoyed keeping it in a plastic jar as a pet for a while.

SPECIES #71

KINGDOM: Animalia
PHYLUM: Arthropoda
CLASS: Arachnida
ORDER: Araneae
FAMILY: Lycosidae
GENUS: *Pardosa*
SPECIES:

Thin-Legged Wolf

Early in our safari we caught this specimen, and I identified it as a **thin-legged wolf spider** from a picture in a reference book. I felt pretty good about my success in identifying it until I learned while doing further research for this book that the thin-legged wolf spider is not the name of the species, but of a genus which includes 520 distinct species! This specimen looks much like *Pardosa milvina*, also known as the shore spider. However, that's just a rough guess based on a few pictures, which is why I've left the species field empty in the taxonomy box.

Thin-legged wolf spiders seem to require moisture and like living in wet areas. Droughts have been known to seriously reduce their numbers here in Ohio.

SPECIES #72

KINGDOM: Animalia
PHYLUM: Arthropoda
CLASS: Insecta
ORDER: Coleoptera
FAMILY: Lampyridae
GENUS: Photinus
SPECIES: pyralis

Lighting the Night

Although we always used to call them lightning bugs, the more common name is firefly. However, they are not really flies, but beetles. There are about 2,000 firefly species worldwide, with about a dozen species in Ohio. The specimen on this page is probably a **big dipper firefly**, also known as the common eastern firefly. The big dipper name has nothing to do with the constellation; rather, it refers to the male's habit of making a big dip in its flight, then flying upward while flashing. If you watch closely, the flight pattern will remind you of a capital J.

Each species of firefly has a different flash pattern. The big dipper firefly flashes about once every six seconds, while others may flash every second or even produce double or triple flashes. The male and female find each other by the pattern and color of the flash. The female crawls on the ground while the male flies and flashes his signal. On the ground, the female firefly sees a flash every second—not her species; a double flash every four seconds—nope; a flash every six seconds—there he is! She flashes back, and the male recognizes the flash and comes looking for his mate.

Most adult fireflies live only a few days, after spending most of their lives as larvae (known as glowworms), crawling in wet places. Thus, most adults do not eat much, if anything. However, adult females of the *Photuris* genus imitate the flash patterns of females of other species to lure males of that species, which they then devour.

Photuris fireflies have an important reason for this behavior. Some fireflies deter attacking predators with a response known as *reflex bleeding,* in which they sweat out a substance laced with toxins called *lucibufagins*. These substances taste horrible and can even kill some attackers, so birds, ants, and spiders tend to leave fireflies alone. However, the *Photuris* fireflies do not naturally produce lucibufagins. By luring and eating male fireflies of other species that do contain the toxins, the female *Photuris* accumulates those toxins in her own blood, protecting both her and her eggs from predators. Once the next generation matures, they must repeat the process to receive continued protection.

I have not included any macro photography of the fireflies. I did catch and dry a few, and I found that firefly abdomens detach themselves from the pronotum, or head, quite easily. Before I knew it, summer was gone, along with the fireflies, and I had no good specimens left to photograph. We never learned whether or not we had more than one species on our property.

The glow from this firefly on our wall is not from its own flash, but a reflection of the camera flash.

SPECIES #73

KINGDOM: Animalia
PHYLUM: Arthropoda
CLASS: Insecta
ORDER: Coleoptera
FAMILY: Elateridae
GENUS:
SPECIES:

Leaping Without Legs

Have you noticed how children sometimes get more fun out of the box than from the fancy toy that came in it? The simple things in life can be fascinating. If you want to give your children a simple toy, give them a **click beetle**. Lay it on its back, and—CLICK!—with a snap and a twist, it flips itself into the air in an attempt to land on its feet. It may need several jumps to land upright.

Actually, this beetle is not exactly a "simple" toy. Its prothorax is hinged to its mesothorax, unlike most beetles. Using a special hook mechanism, click beetles can arch the front and rear parts of their bodies and then release the tension suddenly to flip themselves into the air. They do this to startle and escape from predators and to right themselves when they find themselves on their backs.

Click beetles spend most of their life span—up to three or four years in cold climates—as wireworms. They really are wiry little fellows, and they can become plant pests. Crawling through tiny tunnels in the dirt, wireworms move from plant to plant, nibbling at the roots, and sometimes doing serious damage to crops.

As you may have noticed, I provided neither a genus nor a species name for this specimen. The number of species of click beetles worldwide is pushing 10,000, with nearly a thousand in the United States alone. Most of them are dull in appearance, but what they lack in looks they make up in action.

SPECIES #74

KINGDOM: Animalia
PHYLUM: Arthropoda
CLASS: Insecta
ORDER: Coleoptera
FAMILY: Carabidae
GENUS: *Scarites*
SPECIES: *quadriceps*

Mistaken ID

Our backyard safari sometimes—no, many times!—left us realizing how little we knew about the diversity in our backyard. My first identification of this beetle proved to be wrong. I wrote the article for this species and filled out the species card. But several weeks later, with some help from another source, I learned that this beetle was not a stag beetle after all! Rather, it belongs to the **big-headed ground beetles**, which can look like the stag beetles but are not closely related. Ground beetles tend to live under boards and stones. If you flip a rock and a beetle scurries away, it may be one of these. Beetles compose 40 percent of insect species, with about 40,000 beetle species in the United States alone.

This specimen is a fine example of photo stacking. To get the whole insect in focus required seventy-two photos. At this level of magnification, it would be extremely difficult to capture the whole specimen in focus with just one photo.

If you find a beetle like this, and its antennae segments are longer than they are wide, it is *Scarites quadriceps,* but if the segments are as wide as they are long, it is *S. subterraneus*. Which do you think it is? I propose *quadriceps*.

SPECIES #75

KINGDOM: Animalia
PHYLUM: Arthropoda
CLASS: Insecta
ORDER: Coleoptera
FAMILY: Chrysomelidae
GENUS: *Acalymma*
SPECIES: *vittatum*

Yellow Warning Signs

When you see a yellow sign with black letters, it's usually warning of danger ahead. If you see an insect with those same colors while dawdling through your garden, it may mean the same thing! The **striped cucumber beetle** has a nice paint job but is a dreaded sight to any gardener. Not only does it eat plants, it often carries a pernicious bacteria, *Erwinia tracheiphila*, known as bacterial wilt. Once your cucumber, cantaloupe, or other *cucurbit* plant is infected, nothing but a miracle will cure it. The striped cucumber beetle infects the plant either with its saliva or *frass* (waste), which enters the plant through the leaves damaged by the beetle's chewing.

Striped cucumber beetles have a life cycle of about eight weeks. The first batch appears around the first of July but may not cause noticeable problems. The females lay their little golden-brown eggs on the underside of a leaf, multiplying their numbers by up to twenty times.

Cucumber beetles are attracted to cucurbits because of the chemical *cucurbitacin*, which gives cucurbits their slightly bitter taste. Feeding on cucurbits causes cucurbitacin to accumulate in the beetles' bodies, where it serves as a deterrent to predators. Our Father of details has a lot of secrets in the garden!

Funnel Makers

If you look at the species name, *domestica*, you can probably guess one common name for this spider: domestic house spider. Since they often live in barns, they are also called **barn funnel weavers**, and since they sometimes get stuck in sink drains, they are sometimes called drain spiders. The genus name means "carpet or mat maker."

This spider builds a web shaped like—you guessed it—a funnel. The spider waits in the neck of the funnel until it feels a vibration or sees something hit its web; then it rushes out and grabs its prey before it can untangle itself. The webs are not sticky, so the spider's survival hinges on its quick response. Imagine putting a net outside your door, waiting in the doorway until you feel the vibration of a squirrel on the net, and then rushing out and grabbing the squirrel before it can run away. Welcome to the life of a barn funnel weaver spider!

When you enter an old building and see cobwebs everywhere, in corners and between floor joists and rafters, you are likely seeing the work of barn funnel weavers. While they regularly inhabit human dwellings, they are not a threat to humans. They usually dive into the narrow part of the funnel whenever someone approaches, escaping out a rear exit if they feel too threatened. Since many of these spiders live in heated basements or barns, the females can survive several years, though the males generally live only one year.

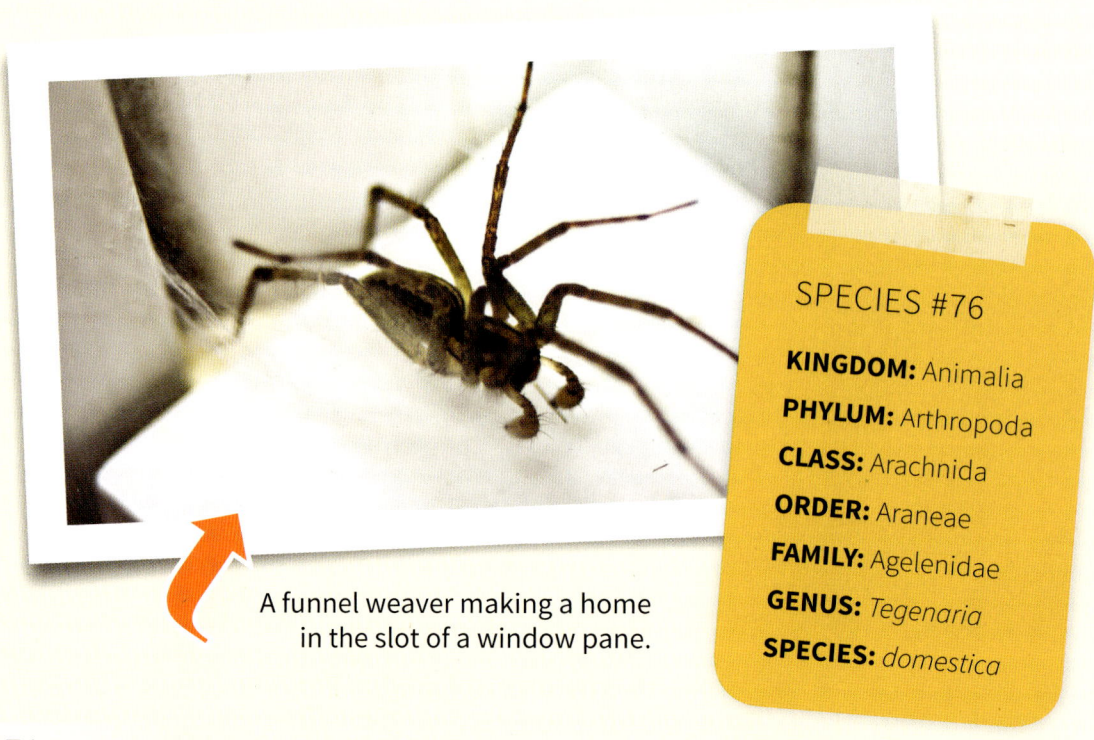

A funnel weaver making a home in the slot of a window pane.

SPECIES #76

KINGDOM: Animalia
PHYLUM: Arthropoda
CLASS: Arachnida
ORDER: Araneae
FAMILY: Agelenidae
GENUS: *Tegenaria*
SPECIES: *domestica*

A funnel weaver "apartment complex" in the basement.

SPECIES #77

KINGDOM: Animalia
PHYLUM: Arthropoda
CLASS: Insecta
ORDER: Coleoptera
FAMILY: Scarabaeidae
GENUS: *Popillia*
SPECIES: *japonica*

Japanese Invasion

If the Colorado potato beetle could pride itself in its pinstripe paint job, the **Japanese beetle** could boast of its metallic sheen. This insect is yet another example of iridescence, that tantalizing glow that our Father of details gives some of His small creatures. The front part shines a deep green, while the rear glows in burnished copper. Why would He adorn a beetle like this? I do not know, unless it is that He loves to exalt the lowly.

Like the Colorado potato beetle, gardeners disapprove of these hungry critters in spite of their attractive appearance. Like potato bugs, Japanese beetles can leave a plant skeletonized. However, in Japan, the land of their origin, natural predators keep their numbers low enough to minimize crop damage.

The first recorded Japanese beetle in the United States was found in New Jersey only a century ago. Today, they have colonized most of the eastern United States and appear set to continue until they reach the Pacific.

If you are looking to rid your garden of these hungry insects, here's a word of caution: Japanese beetle traps may actually draw more beetles to your property than they catch. If you must use a trap, place it away from the plants you want to protect. If you place the trap next to the plants, it will catch a few beetles, but it will attract more, and they will stop to feed on your plants before they enter the trap.

In small numbers, Japanese beetles may be controlled by soapy water (one part dish detergent to four parts water, sprayed directly on the insects). How soap kills insects does not seem to be clearly understood. The most reasonable explanation I found is that soap contains surfactants, which make the water "wetter." This tends to flatten out and coat the insect instead of gathering in droplets. Some sources say this makes the insect "drown"; others say it dehydrates the insect by eating away the outer cell membranes. However it works, soapy water seems to kill certain kinds of insects effectively, and it can work for small numbers of Japanese beetles. If you suffer a massive invasion, you may need to resort to chemical sprays, hand picking, or other methods, in conjunction with soapy water.

If you have Japanese beetles this year, you will most likely see them again next year. The best solace I can suggest for the next time you find these beetles chomping your favorite plant is to take a moment to marvel at the creativity of our Father of details in creating their metallic paint job. Sorry!

Cleanup Crew

If you were a puddle of milk on the breakfast table, this is what a **housefly** would look like. See the sponge in the lower middle of the photo, descending to sop you up? Houseflies cannot bite, since they have no mouth in the ordinary sense of the word. Instead, they slurp liquid food through their "mop." If the food is already liquid, they simply suck it up. If it is solid, like your breakfast toast, they secrete digestive juices and saliva onto the substance, wait a bit while the juices liquefy the food, and then suck it up.

Obviously, the idea of a fly vomiting on our toast then slurping it back up is unappetizing. But worse than that is the possibility that the fly has just fed on some putrid, disease-infested substance five minutes before it began feasting on our toast. When it up-chucks onto the toast to begin digesting your food, guess what else comes out? That's right, its saliva includes whatever disease-causing bacteria are left over from its previous meal. This is an effective way to spread disease, and it's why we don't want houseflies around despite their great service in cleaning up rotting substances. Typhoid, cholera, salmonellosis, bacillary dysentery, and tuberculosis are just a few of the more than one hundred pathogens houseflies can spread.

Houseflies live almost everywhere humans do, and although some 4,000 species of flies exist in the world, houseflies comprise over 90 percent of all flies in human habitations.

SPECIES #78

KINGDOM: Animalia
PHYLUM: Arthropoda
CLASS: Insecta
ORDER: Diptera
FAMILY: Muscida
GENUS: *Musca*
SPECIES: *domestica*

We really stretched our photography capabilities to get this bottom shot of the pulvilli (the yellow pads) of an unknown fly species. This foot is enlarged around 200–300 times. Even so, the hairs on the pad are really too small for the camera to distinguish. Removing the distracting background was difficult, but I think the result is not bad for amateurs!

The housefly has approximately 4,000 lenses in each eye, giving it **omnidirectional** (seeing in all directions at once) vision. With wings that can beat two hundred times per second and the ability to do a ninety-degree turn in about a fifth of a second, they are amazing flying machines. A housefly's top speed is only five miles per hour, but that amounts to three hundred times its own body length every second. For comparison, a jet flying at the speed of sound travels only one hundred times its own length per second. Houseflies can also land upside down on a ceiling. Our Father of details has designed a flying machine many times defter than mankind's best aircraft! Flies are considered the best aerodynamic machines in the world; no other name could honor them better than *fly*.

How do houseflies land and stick on a ceiling? The landing is a mystery to me; the sticking part is easier to understand. On each foot a housefly has two claws, like most insects. In addition, between the housefly's hooks is a **pulvillus**, or pad, that sticks to smooth surfaces using a principle called the **van der Waals force,** a molecular-level attraction which works only over very tiny distances. Each pulvillus has thousands of hairs, each with a flat spot on the end. The hairs ooze a tiny smear of oil, helping them stick to the surface. The whole pad sticks so strongly that, in order to release its foot, the fly actually has to peel it off the surface like Velcro.

A housefly's development from egg to maturity, including complete metamorphosis from maggot to winged adult, takes about two weeks in warm weather. Female flies lay up to nine hundred eggs, and the cycle repeats itself. Were it not for predators, flies would soon be as thick as the plague in Egypt.

Are flies a blessing or a curse? That depends on their population level and where they live. In our houses, we are generally better off without them. But some flies do provide benefits to humans.

The laboratory-raised maggots of some types of blowflies are used by medical doctors to treat infected wounds that won't heal. The maggots eat the dead and rotting flesh without damaging the healthy tissue. At the same time, they release secretions that fight infection and promote faster healing.

Flies are useful in another way. For ninety-five cents, you can buy an ounce of fly larva to use as fishing bait or as food for pet spiders or reptiles.

Our Father of details has perfectly designed the lowly housefly to mop up messes. We usually do not think of flies as being a blessing, but when we take a few minutes to consider them, we can see that they were created with a purpose.

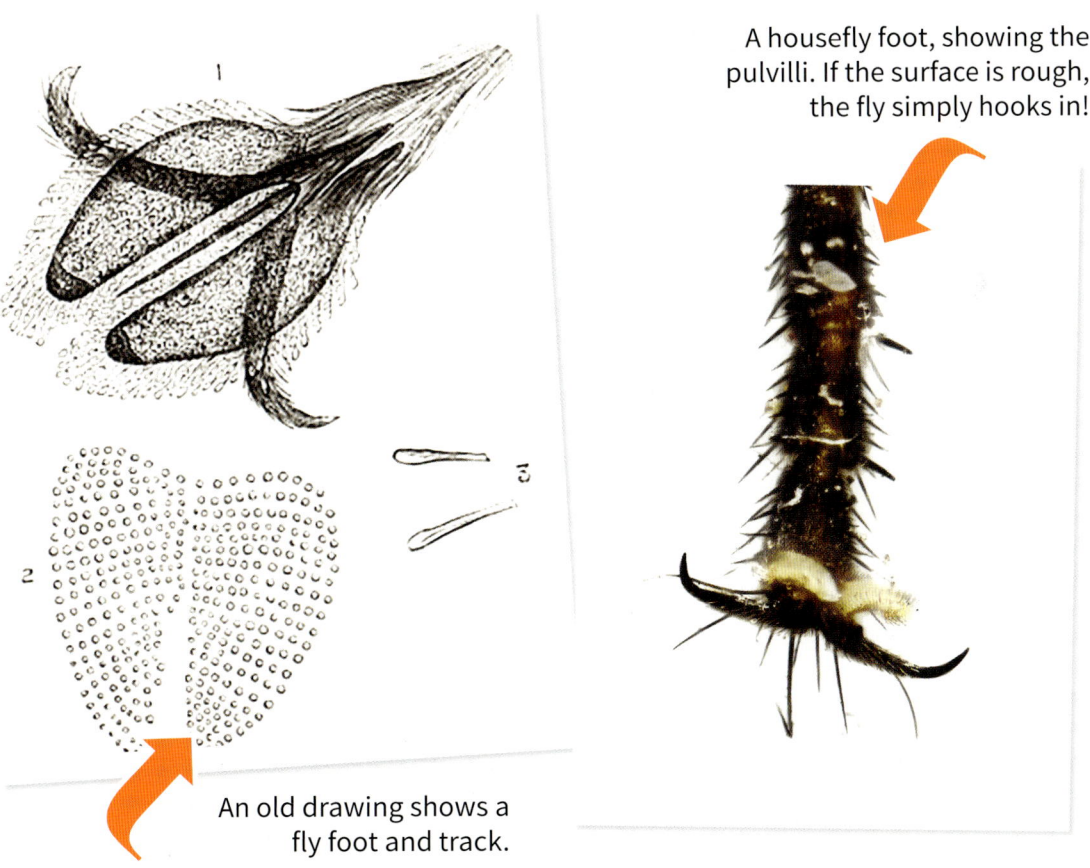

An old drawing shows a fly foot and track.

A housefly foot, showing the pulvilli. If the surface is rough, the fly simply hooks in!

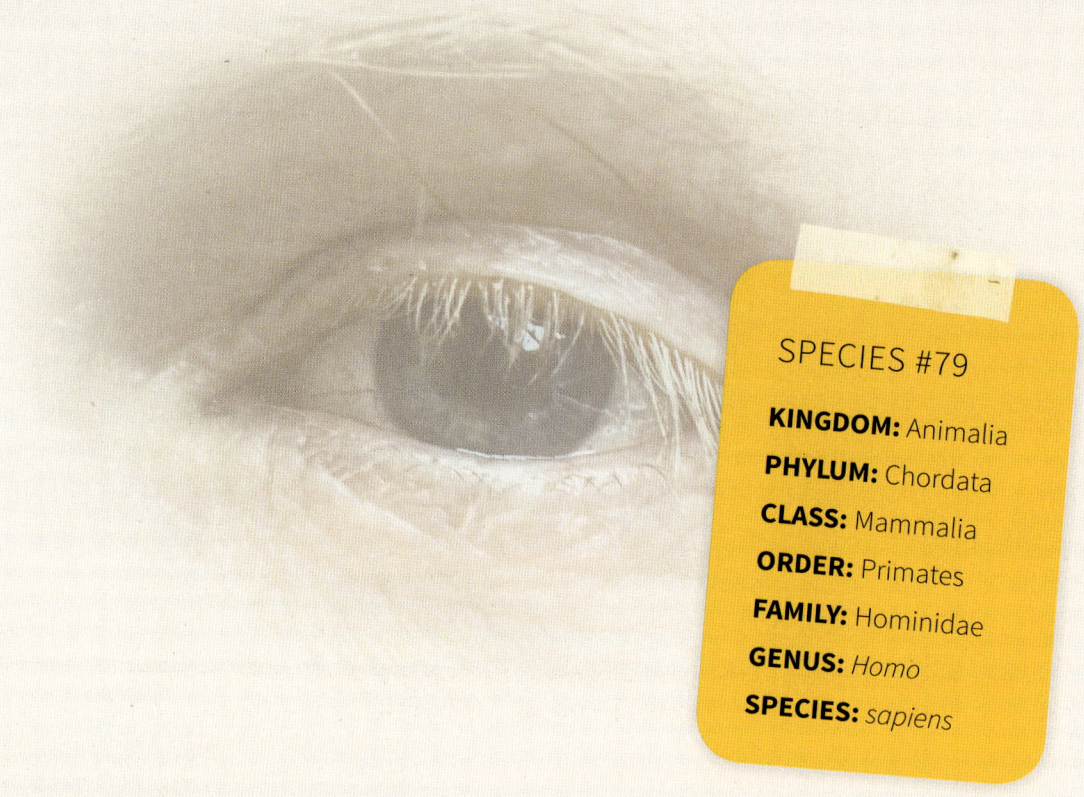

SPECIES #79

KINGDOM: Animalia
PHYLUM: Chordata
CLASS: Mammalia
ORDER: Primates
FAMILY: Hominidae
GENUS: *Homo*
SPECIES: *sapiens*

The Final Species

This journal is not really finished, but we decided to quit. We found nearly 125 species on our safari, and I know we didn't get nearly everything out there. For example, you saw no bees except the bumblebee at the beginning. You saw no wasps, ants, or worms. You saw only a couple of the fly species we captured.

I would guess—and this is just a guess—that we captured only half the species that actually inhabit our two acres. If that guess is correct, there would be about 250 species of fauna. We showed you about eighty species in this journal, roughly a third of what we guess might roam our two acres. Who would have thought there could be 250 species on this "drab" place? What a safari!

I will not leave you without mentioning one final species that roams these two acres. Its eye is pictured above. You guessed it—a human! Yes, that is a photo of my eye. Do you see the hand of our Father of details in that photo? Note that finely-tuned instrument, capable not only of reading books, but also of detecting a whole range of radiation signals. Yes, that eye takes in light waves of various lengths and translates that information to the brain at around a billion impulses per second! If the eye were slower in translating light waves into electrical impulses, my vision would "jump" like an erratic video as it swept across a panoramic view. That eye is auto-focusing, self-cleaning, and auto-adjusting for various light intensities. It is protected by a lightning fast "shutter" and eyebrows. According to some researchers, its resolution is equivalent to a 50-megapixel camera.

Did this all happen by accident as a result of a "big bang"? No, our Father of details created eyes. The design is too purposeful and intricate to be the result of random gene mutations. And the operation of the human eye is just one of the multitude of miracles that happens every day on these two acres. If we were to compare just the eyes of the 250 species on these two acres, how many miraculous, mind-boggling, and majestic marvels would we discover?

We could never describe the multitude of details about the human body in these few paragraphs. That would take another book, or rather a library of books. For now, let's just consider mankind and our place in the universe. Humans are our Father's ultimate creative masterpiece. While some animals outshine humans in certain capacities—we cannot even fly, let alone land upside down like a housefly—we were created to be the dwelling place of the Almighty.

God also gave humans something He gave no other animal—the freedom to choose. Our Father wanted us to love Him, and love is not love unless one chooses to give it freely.

A cicada cannot love God; it is programmed and cannot choose. A comma butterfly cannot love. Even dogs that seem loyal and loving have not really chosen to be that way. Their behaviors are the result of training and conditioning by means of punishments and rewards. No dog ever chose, out of rational forethought, to love someone of its own free will. If a dog's owner treats a dog badly, the dog will not continue to honor that owner.

Humans were created with the power to choose, and God gave us plenty of opportunities to love things besides Him. With the entire world before them, the first man and woman chose to love something other than God, and the results were disastrous! God had to separate Himself from mankind. The character of humanity was corrupted, and the earth itself was cursed as mankind fell captive to Satan's devices. Every descendent of Adam was born with a corrupted nature, self-centered to the core.

It might seem that God failed. He created living beings with a free will so they would choose to love Him, but they chose to love themselves and other created things instead. But God is love, and although His creation had failed and turned away from Him, He was faithful and continued to love His wayward children. Remember, love is a choice. God had every reason to abandon mankind, but He chose to rescue us instead.

For centuries we humans tried to rescue ourselves from the mess we made. Try as we might, nothing could rid us of our oppressive self-centeredness. And as long as we were self-centered, God could not dwell with us. Until self and Satan were overcome, we would remain prisoners. How could this problem be solved?

God, who is rich in mercy and love, was

moved by His eternally righteous character to show justice to those oppressed by sin and Satan. He sent His Son to redeem mankind from spiritual death. The Son came and established a kingdom, a new society of liberated men and women whose character is being restored to the character with which God first created Adam. Jesus accomplished His mission by teaching humans the Father's original intentions for our relationship with Him and each other.

Jesus not only taught us the path of righteous and holy living, but He also provided a way for us to be freed from our destructive habits. He shed His blood so humans could spiritually drink it and have eternal life within them. This blood cleanses us of self-centeredness and empowers us once more to share in the character of our Father. For those who walk with King Jesus, the past is forgiven and the future is redeemed.

Thus the kingdom of heaven on earth began. Since then, men and women from all walks of life, from diverse nations, and from every level of society have found redemption. Partaking in the blood of Jesus, they are freed from Satan and from the power of the old, self-centered nature they inherited from Adam.

Today the earth still groans, awaiting redemption from mankind's sins. The signs of the earth's brokenness are all around us—houseflies now carry horrendous diseases; some female spiders eat the males; many species seem prone to overproduce and become pests.

In God's original world, everything was in harmony, but human sin wreaked havoc. God chose to love us anyway, and now He lays before us a choice: we can choose to love Him, or we can continue on our self-centered way. In His mercy, He has shown us not only the options, but also the future results of either choice. Those who continue to love themselves and this world will remain separated from Him forever, but those who turn to Him, believing in His goodness, are rescued from their corruption and reconciled to Himself through the precious blood of His Son Jesus.

Those who humble themselves and partake of Jesus' blood can be a part of His kingdom, where Satan, self, and sin have been conquered. The kingdom begins here on this troubled earth, corrupted as it is by hatred, gossip, stealing, and even disease-carrying insects. However, God has promised to someday build a new heaven and a new earth. This new heaven and earth will be the eternal home of those who make a simple choice—the choice to love Him, come what may. Have you made that choice?

Appendix A:

A Real Insect Collection

In this journal you have seen our attempts at insect preservation. We were novices, and we remain so. We made oodles of mistakes: breaking legs, drying specimens in crooked positions, and sometimes letting mold overtake our specimens. On this page and the next, we present some photos of a real collection: Anthony Hurst's, at Myerstown Mennonite School, Myerstown, Pennsylvania.[1]

Anthony's collection currently includes more than a thousand specimens. As you can see, it is possible to preserve insects in a beautiful and informative manner. If you are ever in Myerstown, Anthony is happy to let others admire his Father's handiwork, though as of this writing, Anthony lives in Colombia, South America, where he is sharing the Gospel—and capturing South American insects!

---

1 The reflections of the ceiling lights detract from the collection's appearance, but I could not eliminate them when shooting.

Hemiptera

Appendix B:

Science versus Religion?

In today's society, you may hear statements such as, "Science and religion don't mix." Is that true?

Actually, the opposite is closer to the truth: frequently, science and religion cannot be separated. What many people either do not realize or purposely conceal is that all observations, including observations of scientific data, must pass through a human mind—and every human mind has some religious viewpoint.

Some atheists may claim they have no religion, but they are mistaken. Technically speaking, most atheists are *naturalists* (denying the significance of the supernatural)[1] or *materialists* (denying the reality of anything beyond the physical world), and their worldview is colored by these religious views.

Those who believe a supernatural world of non-material spirits exists in conjunction with the natural world are *supernaturalists*. In this camp are many of the world's religions, with widely varying opinions as to how many and what type of spirits exist. Supernaturalists who believe in a creator God

---

[1] *Naturalist* has two meanings; the other, "a student of natural history," simply refers to someone who studies the natural world.

who is involved with the world He has made are known as *theists*. Christians fall into this category.

Worldview Affects Reasoning

What happens when we mix science (the study of the physical world) with religion? Nothing, as long as we never make any judgments or suppositions beyond the raw data. For example, we can look at an insect and determine that it has six legs. No worldview is required for that conclusion. But what if we try to decide *how* or *why* the insect came to have six legs?

At this point our worldview will inevitably color our reasoning process. Theists will assume from the start that God was likely involved at some stage in whatever process gave the insect six legs. By the same token, naturalists will assume from the start that no spiritual forces were involved and will seek a purely natural explanation for the origin of the insect's legs.

Because they believe the spiritual world does not exist, or that it does not affect this world, naturalists ignore it, and they are left to explain the physical world with only the data the current physical world can offer. Unfortunately, some naturalists have deceived themselves into thinking that their worldview does not color their interpretation of scientific data.

Why do naturalists ignore the spiritual world? There is no easy answer. Many have simply been taught by books and teachers that the spiritual world is not real, and they believed what they were told. Others seem to deny the existence of the supernatural world because they do not want to be subject to it. If you have been told God requires a moral or ethical standard of conduct from mankind, one way to avoid obeying is to declare that God does not exist. In this way you become your own god, allowing you to ignore God's moral standard without troubling your conscience as easily.

The Natural Cannot See the Supernatural

Some people deny the supernatural world because they have not been able to find it with the tools of science. But how could devices designed to measure the natural world ever determine whether or not the supernatural exists? Only spiritual "tools" can detect the supernatural.

To say that the supernatural does not exist because it cannot be detected with the scientific method is like a blind man declaring that light does not exist. Since he cannot observe light waves with his senses, do they not exist? No, we are wiser than that. But this is the same mistake made by the person who declares that the supernatural world does not exist because he cannot find it using natural measuring tools.

The Big Bang and Religion

For an example of how a worldview colors the results of science, let's consider the Big Bang. The raw data seems to indicate that the universe is expanding on all sides of us at an ever-increasing rate. Assuming that this data is accurate, what does it tell us about the origins of the universe? What does it say about how our earth came into existence? What does it tell us about life 5,000 years ago? By itself, the raw data tells us absolutely nothing. All we really know is that the universe appears to be expanding.

Based on his worldview, a naturalist might interpret this data by dividing the size of the universe by the rate of expansion to estimate how long it has been expanding.[2] Thus, the naturalist determines that some billions of years ago the universe started from a central point, before which it did not exist. That point is known as the Big Bang, but does that prove that the Big Bang certainly happened? No. The Big Bang is the result of one interpretation of the data, filtered through the worldview of the scientists involved.

If we look at the data from a Christian worldview, it is the same data—the universe still appears to be expanding rapidly on all sides of us. Once again, the data alone tells us nothing about the origins of the universe. But a Christian believes there is a supernatural force, whom we call God, with the power to control the forces of the physical universe. God may have started the universe at near its current size. He may have slowed down, sped up, stopped, or reversed the growth of the universe at any time in history. Thus, the evidence we can see in the present cannot give us certainty about the past.

However, this God has actually spoken to mankind, and He has told us certain details of the origin of the universe. He indicates that He personally created the universe within the past few thousand years. He has not told us the details of how He accomplished that, nor what size the universe was immediately after Creation, nor its initial rate of expansion. Unless He reveals those things, we will never know for sure, since raw scientific data is not available for that time period.

Naturalists would probably say such an interpretation amounts to "mixing science and religion." What they do not admit is that their own interpretation of the data (the Big Bang theory) is also a mixture of science and their religion—the religion of naturalism that denies any supernatural involvement in the universe. Although many who hold such a worldview have convinced themselves that they have no religion, they actually worship human intelligence and reasoning. Self-interpretation is the foundation of this religion, and this prophet demands that all mankind bow before him. As Christians, we need to recognize the voice of this false prophet and open our spiritual eyes and ears to the truth. He that hath ears to hear, let him hear![3]

---

2 This example is simplified for the purpose of the illustration; in reality, the calculations used by astronomers to estimate the age of the universe are far more complex than this.

3 Matthew 11:15

Photo credits

All photos are by Mike or Daniel Atnip, with the following exceptions:

4–7 Space and earth photos: Public domain.
  23 Monarch butterflies in trees: Luís Ávalos / CC-BY-SA-3.0 /.
  33 Inch worm: G. Bohne / CC-BY-SA-2.0.
  43 Helicoverpa zea moth: Public domain from Wikipedia.
  44 Southern hawker dragonfly molting: Böhringer Friedrich / CC-BY-SA-3.0.
  66 Spider anatomy: John Henry Comstock and Ryan Wilson / CC-BY-SA-3.0.
  67 Spider eyes: drawings based on diagram from www.spiders.us/articles/identification/. Used by permission.
  72 Cricket dish photo: Wikimedia Commons User: Takeaway / CC-BY-SA-3.0.
109 Quesadilla photo: Gunnar Wolf / Wikimedia Commons / CC-BY-SA-3.0.
126 Large maple spanworm caterpillar: Gyorgy Csoka / CC-BY-SA-3.0.
134 Rust mite: Public domain photo by USDA.
136 Book Lung drawing: Public domain drawing by John Henry Comstock, 1912.
136 Spiracle valve photo: Wikipedia User: Chsh / CC-BY-SA-3.0.
146 Crane fly drawing: Charles Thomas Brues / Public Domain.
149 Giant leopard moth: Wikipedia User: Kevincollins123 / CC BY-SA 3.0.
151 Slug body parts diagram: Wikipedia User: Billion / CC BY-SA 3.0.
181 Fly foot drawing: Public domain by J. E. Rombouts, 1884.

See https://creativecommons.org/licenses/by-sa/3.0/deed.en for information on Creative Commons licenses.

About Our Photos

It's been said that a good photographer shows 10 percent of his work, while an excellent photographer shows 1 percent. The point is that getting one excellent photo requires taking ninety-nine that would not impress your friends. In collecting photos for this book, we clicked our shutter an estimated 15,000 times!

Most of those shutter clicks involved a process known as focus stacking. The higher the magnification of a lens, the less its depth of field, or the shallower the area it can focus on. When taking really closeup photos, our depth of field was in the thousandths of an inch. That meant that if we wanted to get an object one inch thick in focus all the way from the front to the back, we would need to take hundreds of photos, moving the camera forward several thousandths of an inch each time.

For example, the fly foot on page 181 is about .005–.010 inch thick. To get every part of the foot in focus, Daniel took forty-two photos. We then took those forty-two photos and processed them through image stacking software, which took the focused part of each image and stacked them together, discarding all parts of the image not in focus. The result is one image, in focus all the way from front to rear.

Above is a photo of our camera with a 10X microscope objective mounted on the front, which is how we managed to get the closest photos. The left photo shows the dial on the translation stage the camera is mounted on. A one-degree turn would move the camera forward approximately .0001 inch. On a typical high-magnification shoot, we would turn the dial ten degrees for each photo in a stack.

Our safari was not only into the world of animal life, but also into the realm of light and color and how to fine-tune them to produce a good photo. As you can see from this journal, myriads of details remain for us to explore.

Glossary

androconia (singular: androconium) – The unique scales on certain male butterflies that emit odors, often to attract females.

apulmonates – Animals that have no lungs.

basitarsi (singular: basitarsum) – The leg sections right above the "ankle" of an insect. In humans, this would be equivalent to the lower leg.

book lungs – Lungs stacked beside each other like the pages of a book, similar in appearance to the gills on a fish, but different in that they take oxygen from air, not water.

cerci (singular: cercus) – Paired appendages on the rear of some insects. They are not tails as such, but can appear as a double tail.

chelicerae (singular: chelicera) – The "jaws" of a spider, often tipped with a set of fangs. (See the blue-green chelicerae on page 37 for a clear example.)

chitin – A hardened polymer made of sucrose. This compound is what forms the hard parts of insects, including their wings.

cryoprotectant – A substance produced in some animals to keep tissue from freezing. It is an antifreeze, but not the same substance used to keep water in engines from freezing.

cucurbit (short for Cucurbitaceae) – A plant family consisting of squash, gourds, melons, cucumbers, and similar plants.

cucurbitacin – The chemical compound found in cucurbits that gives them a "bitter" taste.

diapause – The state of dormancy that some animals enter, initiated by bad weather or other adverse conditions. Many insects survive through the cold winter months by this method. Similar to hibernation.

dichoptic – Eyesight with two independent fields of view in the eyes.

diurnal – Relating to the daytime, as opposed to *nocturnal*.

elytra (singular: elytron) – The hardened forewings of some insects (beetles, for example). Elytra serve more for a protective covering of the rear wings than they do for flight.

exoskeleton – An exterior skeleton,

as found in insects, as opposed to the *endoskeleton* (interior skeleton) found in mammals.

frass – Insect excrement; manure.

glucosinolates – The "smelly" oils in plants related to mustard.

halteres – The knobbed balancing organs of certain flying insects that replace what would otherwise be the rear wings.

hemimetabolous – Incomplete (literally, "halfway") metamorphosis. The specimen will change appearance, but not a total change as from a caterpillar to a butterfly. Compare with *holometabolous*.

hemolymph – The "blood" of insects and spiders. This is not the same as our blood, but serves the same basic purpose of transporting substances throughout the body.

hermaphrodites – Animals or plants having both male and female reproductive organs.

holometabolous – Complete metamorphosis, where the specimen is drastically changed in function and appearance. Compare with *hemimetabolous*.

holoptic – Having the eyes so close together that they are almost like one single eye.

hydrophobia – Literally, "the fear of water." However, the term *hydrophobic* is also used of substances that have no attraction to water and appear to repulse water. In other words, water does not "stick" to the substance.

imago – An adult insect.

instar – An insect or spider in any of the stages of development in between the various molts as it grows into an adult. The number of instars varies with the species.

iridescent – Showing colors like those of a rainbow, usually depending on the angle of sight.

lucibufagins – Horrible-tasting steroid pheromones released by some animals. These serve as a deterrent to predators.

materialists – Those who deny that anything exists beyond the physical world. They are the opposite of *supernaturalists*.

mycelium (can be singular or plural, although *mycelia* is sometimes used for the plural) – The thread-like hairs of a fungus that spread through the host. Although they are not roots as such, they look and act like the roots of a plant.

naturalists – Those who deny the significance of the spiritual world; very similar to *materialists*.

nocturnal – Relating to the nighttime; opposite of *diurnal*.

ocelli (singular: ocellus) – Simple eyes that some invertebrates have. These are often located between the compound eyes of insects.

ommatidia (singular: ommatidium) – The individual units that make up a compound eye.

omnidirectional – "In all directions." This term is used for animals that have enough eyes or a large enough compound eye to see in all directions at once.

osmeterium (plural: osmeteria) – A horn-like protrusion on some caterpillars that emits a terrible stench to ward off predators.

ovipositor – The organ at the tail end of some insects that deposits the eggs. Literally, the word means "egg positioner."

pheromones – Chemicals released by some animals to "communicate" with others of the same species.

proboscis – The protruding mouth parts of insects. Sometimes called the nose, but the function is more like that of the mouth of mammals.

pronotum (plural: pronota) – The plate-like structure that covers the upper part (the back, if the insect were to stand on two legs) of the thorax of insects.

puddling – The habit of some butterflies to gather at a damp location (a puddle, for example) and suck up the moisture in large volumes to gather out the nutrients.

pulmonates – Having lungs or lung-like organs.

pulvillus (plural: pulvilli) – The hairy pad on the foot of some insects, used to "stick" to smooth surfaces.

radii (singular: radius) – Lines extending from the center of a circle to the edges. In spider webs, the radii hold the circular parts together.

reflex bleeding – Also known as *autohaemorrhaging*. The action of "bleeding" out chemicals that are distasteful, putrid, or even toxic as a form of self-defense.

safari – A Swahili word, derived from Arabic, which means "a journey or expedition."

speciation – The formation or development of new species.

spinnerets – The organs on spiders and caterpillars for spinning silky threads.

spiracle valve – The openings in some animals that lead to the respiratory system. These valves can usually open and close completely, unlike our human nose.

stabilimentum (plural: stabilimenta) – The "decoration" on some spider webs that some believe are used to stabilize the web. The actual use of stabilimenta is disputed.

stridulate – The rubbing of body parts together to create sound.

subimago – The instar before the final adult in mayflies. It may look like the adult except with immature wings or no wings at all.

supernaturalists – Those who believe in the existence of a supernatural world, in contrast to *naturalists and materialists*.

tarsi (singular: tarsus) – The "ankle" segments of a foot.

theists – Those who believe in a God who is

actively involved in the world.

tracheal system – The breathing system of insects, composed of fine, air-filled tubes that branch throughout the body.

tymbal – In certain insects, the vibrating membrane by which they make sound. Similar in function to a stretched drum skin.

tympanum (plural: tympana) – The external hearing structure of certain insects and other animals.

van der Waals force – In chemistry, the attraction or repulsion between molecules. This attraction is used by some animal feet to "stick" to otherwise slick surfaces.

Index of Species

B
banded garden spider 122
barn funnel weaver 174
big dipper firefly 167
big-headed ground beetle 170
bold jumping spider 37
brown rove beetle 100

C
cabbage white butterfly 52
Carolina grasshopper 18
cedar beetle 156
Chinese mantis 103
click beetle 169
clouded sulphur butterfly 50
Colorado potato beetle 129
common fruit fly 114
corn earworm 43
corn smut 109
crane flies 89

D
Davis's tree cricket 133
differential grasshopper 48
dog flea 26

E
eastern comma butterfly 143

F
fall field cricket 70
fishing spider 135
furrow orb weaver 152

G
geometer moth 33
giant leopard moth 148
grass spider 144

H
harnessed tiger moth 108
harvestmen 80
housefly 178

I
Isabella tiger moth 56

J
Japanese beetle 177
June bug 117

L

ladybird beetle 85
large maple spanwood moth 126
large yellow underwing 97
long-jawed orb weaver 120

M

mayfly 106
micromoths 101
monarch butterfly 22
mosquitoes 160

N

net-wing beetle 110
nitrous bonnet 82

O

orange marbled orb weaver 124
orchard spider 131

P

phantom crane fly 146
poison ivy leaf gall mite 132
praying mantis 104

R

red admiral butterfly 64

S

scissor grinder locust 30
slugs 150
soldier fly 155
southern scurfy Quaker moth 112
spiny-bellied orb weaver 69
striped cucumber beetle 173
sweet potato weevil 121

T

thin-legged wolf spider 165
tiger swallowtail 25
two-spotted tree cricket 159

V

Virginia creeper sphinx moth 75
Virginia tiger moth 56

W

wolf spiders 78

Z

zebra jumping spider 36

About the Author

During the writing of this book, Mike Atnip, his wife Ellen, and their son Daniel lived in New Bedford, Ohio. Mike grew up among the cornfields of east-central Indiana, tromping through the fields and woods on a regular basis. Ellen grew up in southeast Pennsylvania, at the foot of Blue Mountain, but later lived in northern New York where the snow blows deep. Daniel was adopted from the tall Andes Mountains in Bolivia, South America, but has spent most of his life in the United States.

The Atnip family hopes that people young and old will see God's glory, power, and love in the creation of so many marvelous forms of life, and submit their hearts to Him as to a loving Father and Friend.

Mike welcomes reader response and can be contacted at atnips@gmail.com. You may also write to him in care of Christian Aid Ministries, P.O. Box 360, Berlin, Ohio 44610.

Christian Aid Ministries

Christian Aid Ministries was founded in 1981 as a nonprofit, tax-exempt 501(c)(3) organization. Its primary purpose is to provide a trustworthy and efficient channel for Amish, Mennonite, and other conservative Anabaptist groups and individuals to minister to physical and spiritual needs around the world. This is in response to the command "... do good unto all men, especially unto them who are of the household of faith" (Galatians 6:10).

Each year, CAM supporters provide approximately 15 million pounds of food, clothing, medicines, seeds, Bibles, Bible story books, and other Christian literature for needy people. Most of the aid goes to orphans and Christian families. Supporters' funds also help to clean up and rebuild for natural disaster victims, put up Gospel billboards in the U.S., support several church-planting efforts, operate two medical clinics, and provide resources for needy families to make their own living. CAM's main purposes for providing aid are to help and encourage God's people and bring the Gospel to a lost and dying world.

CAM has staff, warehouses, and distribution networks in Romania, Moldova, Ukraine, Haiti, Nicaragua, Liberia, and Israel. Aside from management, supervisory personnel, and bookkeeping operations, volunteers do most of the work at CAM locations. Each year, volunteers at our warehouses, field bases, Disaster Response Services projects, and other locations donate over 200,000 hours of work.

CAM's ultimate purpose is to glorify God and help enlarge His kingdom. "... whatsoever ye do, do all to the glory of God" (1 Corinthians 10:31).

The Way to God and Peace

We live in a world contaminated by sin. Sin is anything that goes against God's holy standards. When we do not follow the guidelines that God our Creator gave us, we are guilty of sin. Sin separates us from God, the source of life.

Since the time when the first man and woman, Adam and Eve, sinned in the Garden of Eden, sin has been universal. The Bible says that we all have "sinned and come short of the glory of God" (Romans 3:23). It also says that the natural consequence for that sin is eternal death, or punishment in an eternal hell: "Then when lust hath conceived, it bringeth forth sin: and sin, when it is finished, bringeth forth death" (James 1:15).

But we do not have to suffer eternal death in hell. God provided forgiveness for our sins through the death of His only Son, Jesus Christ. Because Jesus was perfect and without sin, He could die in our place. "For God so loved the world that he gave his only begotten Son, that whosoever believeth in him should not perish, but have everlasting life" (John 3:16).

A sacrifice is something given to benefit someone else. It costs the giver greatly. Jesus was God's sacrifice. Jesus' death takes away the penalty of sin for everyone who accepts this sacrifice and truly repents of their sins. To repent of sins means to be truly sorry for and turn away from the things we have done that have violated God's standards (Acts 2:38; 3:19).

Jesus died, but He did not remain dead. After three days, God's Spirit miraculously raised Him to life again. God's Spirit does something similar in us. When we receive Jesus as our sacrifice and repent of our sins, our hearts are changed. We become spiritually alive! We develop new desires and attitudes (2 Corinthians 5:17). We begin to make choices that please God (1 John 3:9). If we do fail and commit sins, we can ask God for forgiveness. "If we confess our sins, he is faithful and just to forgive us our sins, and to cleanse us from all unrighteousness" (1 John 1:9).

Once our hearts have been changed, we want to continue growing spiritually. We will be happy to let Jesus be the Master of our lives and will want to become more like Him. To do this, we must meditate on God's Word and commune with God in prayer. We will testify to others of this change by being baptized and sharing the good news of God's victory over sin and death. Fellowship with a faithful group of believers will strengthen our walk with God (1 John 1:7).